THE MOST IMPORTANT PERSON OF OUR TIME

THE MOST IMPORTANT PERSON OF OUR TIME

EBENEZER AGBOOLA

The Agboola Ministries

The Most Important Person of Our Time
Copyright © 2020 by Ebenezer Agboola

All rights reserved. No part of this book may be reproduced in any manner whatsoever without written permission except in the case of brief quotations embodied in critical articles and reviews.

First Printing, 2020

Scripture quotations are taken from the Holy Bible, New Living Translation, copyright ©1996, 2004, 2007, 2013, 2015 by Tyndale House Foundation. Used by permission of Tyndale House Publishers, Inc., Carol Stream, Illinois 60188. All rights reserved.

Scripture quotes marked (KJV) are taken from the King James Version of the Bible.
Scripture quotes marked (NKJV) are taken from the New King James Version, Copyright © 1982 Thomas Nelson. All rights reserved.

Scripture quotes marked (ESV) are taken from the ESV® Bible (The Holy Bible, English Standard Version®) copyright © 2001 by Crossway Bibles,

Scripture quotes marked (ISV) are taken from the Holy Bible: International Standard Version® Release 2.1. Copyright © 1996-2012 The ISV Foundation. ALL RIGHTS RESERVED INTERNATIONALLY.

Scriptures quotes marked (AMP) are taken from the Holy Bible: Amplified Bible. Copyright © 2015 by The Lockman Foundation, La Habra, CA 90631. All rights reserved.

Scriptures quotes marked (CEV) are taken from the Holy Bible: Contemporary English Version®. Copyright © 1995 American Bible Society. All rights reserved.

Any people depicted in stock imagery provided by Thinkstock are models, and such images are being used for illustrative purposes only.

ISBN: 978-1-7775-0290-4 (sc)
ISBN: 978-1-7775-0291-1 (e)

Cover Design by Kaiha Marah.

Contents

Dedication	vi
Acknowledgement	vii
Foreword	ix
Introduction	xi
1 Hold Up...Before We Go	1
2 The Identity	12
3 Who is the God of this Age?	49
4 The God of this Age	65
5 Understanding the God of this Age	84
6 Growth and Sustenance	146
7 Conclusion	159
Contact the Author	165
About the Book	167
About The Author	169

To the triune God. You are the author; I return all the glory back to you.

Father, You are the One who was, who is and is to come. You made this book a reality despite all the resistance. I am perpetually grateful for Your unconditional love.

My Lord and Savior, Jesus, You are the reason I am saved and received access to the mysteries in this book. I am eternally indebted to Your work on the cross of Calvary.

My ever-present help, the Holy Spirit, it is literally impossible to quantify Your dependable help and unending awesomeness. You inspired me and released the grace to bring this book to fruition. You make complex things very simple. Thank You for the dictates of the supernatural and Your divine leading.

Acknowledgement

Excellence is the hallmark of God. So, when God calls an individual for a purpose, He provides everything that the individual will need for excellence. For this reason, Jesus called many disciples to bring about the excellencies of God through the ministry of salvation. Hence the help of God-ordained people is a vital ingredient for excellent results. I would like to take this opportunity to acknowledge such individuals that God has placed in my life for His call.

Victor Owunne, your proclivity for rigour is amazing. Thank you for your insights and professionalism. Your drive for excellence is a great gift from God. I know that being the first editor can be challenging, but you came through by the help of God. I am grateful to God for His gifts in you and His hand upon you.

Pastor Emmanuel Adewusi, my spiritual father. What can I say? The word of God says in Jeremiah 3:15 (NLT), *"And I will give you shepherds after my own heart, who will guide you with knowledge and understanding."* Thank you for being a fulfilment of this scripture to me and others. I thank God for His grace in your life.

Tumininu Agboola, my lovely wife. You have been there from the very first book. I am grateful to God for the grace He has conferred on you. I praise God that you discovered His editorial gift in your life. Your willingness and pursuit of excellence is something I cherish. Thank you for your encouragement and support. I am grateful to God for giving you to me; I love you.

Kaiha Marah, I am grateful for the gift of God in your life. Thank you for your tireless effort in the design elements of this book.

Foreword

If there is anyone, we should be focusing our attention on as a church at this time in history, that divine personality is definitely the Holy Spirit. The Holy Spirit was the only one who could transform Peter from a fearful person to a bold and fiery preacher. Even though Peter already spent time with the Word (Jesus Christ), he remained fearful until he personally encountered the Holy Spirit. Jesus Christ also needed the Holy Spirit before He could fulfill His mission on the earth. When it was time for Jesus to kick off His ministry of restoration and transformation, He was baptized in the Holy Spirit at the Jordan River. I took the instruction of Jesus Christ to His disciples about remaining in Jerusalem for the enduement of power from above to heart, when our ministry was about to start. I spent time to ensure I was empowered for the ministry journey ahead of me, and I am determined to remain in fellowship with the Holy Spirit all through my assignment. You might be wondering why you need a relationship with the Holy Spirit if you are not in ministry. In addition to being able to dominate the spiritual realm, the modern-day believer in the marketplace will need the Holy Spirit in order to compete favorably in an artificial Intelligence and robot-dominated world.

While no one can claim to know all there is to know about the Holy Spirit, this book does shed a lot of light on that divine personality. For anyone to productively engage with the Holy Spirit, knowledge and experience are needed. This book will provide you with the knowledge you need to begin your exploration or enhance your already existent relationship with the Holy Spirit. The knowledge received but not practiced will do no good. I encourage you to read this book with an open mind, heart, and in conjunction with the word of God and strive to apply its content.

May God bless you richly.

Pastor Emmanuel Adewusi
Cornerstone Christian Church of God

Introduction

According to Geology, the age of the earth is over 4 billion years old. Over the time span of the earth's existence, many people have come and gone, and there has been a plethora of civilizations and technological advancements over the ages. A few days ago, I was going over an article that listed some items, which individuals born in the year 2020 will never get to experience. Antiquated technologies have given way to the emergence of modern technologies, to ease the human way of life. Some of these technological evolutions have been good while some have posed negative impacts.

A notable attribute that is conspicuous, with regards to changes across time spans, is population. Prior to the cusp of the industrial revolution, a large family was enviable, because of its benefits in farm labor; however, the mechanization of farming tools has led to reforms in human desires for large family sizes.

Time Magazine, among many other magazines, routinely lists influential people; but one strange thing about this is that the names of these individuals change; year after year, decade after decade. This simply means, "change is constant."

Stephen Harper was the prime minister of Canada for nearly a decade; today, Justin Trudeau is the prime minister of Canada. The fact is, the moment a person is dethroned, they might become irrelevant and unimportant.

It is clear that if we are going to make it in this day and age, a relationship with those in charge is crucial. The question remains, "If these people of influence are changing at a moment's notice, what is the strategy to ensure we are always where we ought to be?"

Do you know there is a person whose years have no end? Do you know there is a person who reigns supreme and does not change? This is the person introduced in this book. Knowing this person is the only hope of being who we are meant to be in this ever-changing world. Here is a fact, there are many ways to the top, but there is a guaranteed way to the top; this way is what will be discussed in this book. You are going to learn about the most important person of this time and all time. The only one, who was, who is and is to come. Knowing Him will set you on the course for greatness, and cultivating an intimate relationship with Him will keep you moving higher and higher. What's more to say? If there is such a person out there, I want to know about Him. What about you?

Buckle up, fasten your seat belt and let us learn about the most important person of our time.

1

Hold Up...Before We Go

As we journey through this book, it is important that we properly chart our course and fix our eyes on the prize. Understanding the rules of this journey is crucial and important to our end result; these rules are encompassed by this chapter. Though this book is about the most important person, the principles covered in this chapter are the foundation of this book.

On Your Marks: The Wisdom Recipe

Wisdom is the principal thing; therefore, get wisdom. And in all your getting, get understanding. (**Proverbs 4:7 NKJV**)

Wisdom is essential to have and live a successful life. A person who has wisdom is deemed wise; a person who lacks wisdom is deemed foolish. This connotes that wisdom is what separates the wise from the foolish, and the successful from the unsuccessful. Just like every success story, there are responsibilities that must be assumed by any individual who seeks success. When those responsibilities are properly undertaken, such an individual is deemed wise and can attain success. I refer to those responsibilities as *"the recipe for wisdom."*

After denoting wisdom as important (*the principal thing*), the scripture above continued by adding another vital virtue to the mix (*And in all your getting, get **understanding***). Understanding was introduced after wisdom; why? It is clear to me that the author of this scripture (which is God—**2 Timothy 3:16**) is telling us that these two virtues are connected. Furthermore, the tone with which the latter part of this scripture was written suggests the significance of both virtues. However, understanding is the prerequisite for wisdom. Yes, wisdom is important, but we need understanding to attain wisdom. Consequently, understanding is our responsibility and hence the prerequisite and recipe for wisdom.

Get Set: Get Understanding

Now let us zoom in on the recipe of wisdom. In the latter part of **Proverbs 4:7**, the Bible made it crystal clear that getting understanding is our responsibility. This obviously raises the question: what is understanding and how do I get it?

According to Google, to understand is *"to perceive the intended meaning of a thing."* While this is accurate, I define understanding as knowing the *"why"* of a thing—in this context, a thing refers to facts or information. It is often said that *"those that know-how will always work for those that know why."*

Information in itself is insufficient, even though it is important. The individuals with information are those that know the how. Whereas, knowing the "*why*" is absolutely contingent on gaining understanding. For instance, there are people who have refused to drive or own a car, even though they are knowledgeable about its functionalities. On the other hand, there are people who are inexperienced in the functionalities of a car but are well versed in its benefits as a necessity.

Our actions and reactions are the resultants of our answer to the question "why." Have you ever seen a brilliant person who is struggling in certain areas of their life? You might look at such a person and wonder, what is going on? Some of us might even advise them to get it together. To be honest, some people are genuinely making efforts, but they need to understand the "why," to obtain any type of breakthrough. The "how" restricts a person to a specific application, while the "why" opens up doors for copious applications. Without the "why," we only have information but not understanding. To put this in perspective, I will like to use a concept that is common to students—cramming. If a student crams for an exam on a preceding night, they are unconsciously hoping to see exam questions that align with what they crammed. If any misalignment is encountered by the student, it can lead to their failure in the exam. However, if a student studies assiduously and understands the concepts (that is, the why) in good time, they will not care about twists in exam questions, they will also perform well in the exam. This is because the understanding gained from studying also infuses the requisite confidence to pass the exam. I have heard many people say, "I don't like math." The truth remains that mathematics is not difficult; it is simply the application of proven formulas to solve problems. Honestly, I believe anybody can excel in math. However, the deficiency in understanding math concepts has driven many individuals to fail and dislike math. Yes, it is good to go to class, but this in itself is not enough to pass the class. There are students who skip classes because they believe they are not learning anything. However, they commit themselves to studying on their own and they still pass the class. A student who doesn't know the why of the information being provided during classes will always be susceptible to the twist and turn of any exam, which can culminate in failure.

As part of the definition for understanding, we noticed that information (also known as knowledge) was introduced as the recipe. In simple terms, the prerequisite for success is wisdom; and the prerequisite for wisdom is understanding. Without information, there can be no understanding. Hence information gathering is essential for gaining understanding and attaining success. If we want to adhere to the advice of the Bible, to get understanding, then we must gather information and assimilate it to enable understanding.

Understanding Recipe: Knowledge

The definition of "Knowledge," in google is simply facts and information. These are the raw materials that must be processed to obtain success as an end result. This simply means that not all information will be useful and valuable. Keeping that in mind, the source of information matters. The integrity of information is dependent on the source of information. When we appropriately position ourselves for the right information, the processing phase becomes easy; the useless and non-valuable information will be filtered out. The processing phase is where understanding is acquired.

Once we gain an understanding of the information we have acquired, we are capacitated to apply it to the right situation. Hence wisdom puts us on the roadmap of success. If we are struggling in any area of life, the simple answer is that we lack the understanding needed for wisdom in that area of life. Though we might have all the knowledge, the real question that we must always answer is the "why."

Get Set: Understanding is Light

For every command of the Bible, there is an implication in the spirit. This is because we are spirit beings. Every action and reaction we engage in has an impact on our spiritual life. Understanding is no exception, because getting understanding is important and also an instruction of the Bible.

In the words of my spiritual father, "we are represented as light in the spirit realm". This was confirmed by Jesus in **Matthew 5:14 NLT** (*You are the light of the world--like a city on a hilltop that cannot be hidden*). Like many other words of Jesus, this scripture is somewhat a metaphor. It is not talking about a literal city here, but illustrating what we look like in the spirit realm. For example, if we are looking at Toronto from deep space at night, all that can be seen of that city is its lights. And depending on how far above the earth we are, these lights would simply be seen as a dot.

As you know, there are different sources of light. And with these different sources come different intensities. Furthermore, different exposures to different sources of light create differences in brightness. This is a genuine connotation of who we are as children of God. The light we emit in the spirit realm evinces our understanding in the physical realm. Our level of understanding is directly proportional to the intensity of our light, and our brightness is directly proportional to our exposure to the light of Jesus Christ. Therefore, the light we carry is the level of our understanding.

This was one of the reasons the Bible advises us to get understanding in **Proverbs 4:7**. The devil is associated with darkness (**Colossians 1:13 NLT**: *For he has rescued us from the kingdom of darkness and transferred us into the Kingdom of his dear Son*). He thrives when things are hidden or unknown, because then and only then can he deceive. The kingdom of darkness is filled with darkness and the devil is the king. Do not forget that his only trick is deception, and its success is contingent on some information staying hidden. Note that the devil lies a lot and he is the master of deceits (**John 8:44 NLT**: *For you are the children of your father the devil, and you love to do the evil things he does. He was a murderer from the beginning. He has always hated the truth because there is no truth in him. When he lies, it is consistent with his character; for he is a liar and the father of lies.*).

Understanding connotes what you know and get; therefore, it brings illumination (i.e., light) both physically and spiritually. With understanding, you have the sense for action without restriction. You know exactly what to do. Clarity (i.e., wisdom) is available. Therefore, understanding is light and lack of it is darkness. In **Psalm 119:104-105 NLT** (*Your commandments give me **understanding**; no wonder I hate every false* *way of life. Your word is a **lamp** to guide my feet and a **light** for my path.)* and **Psalm 119:130 NLT** (*The teaching of your word gives **light**, so even the simple can **understand**)*, the Bible confirms the principle of understanding as light. It is important that I explain here that some parts of the scripture were written to be interpreted systematically. Oftentimes, when the Bible talks about something right after another such as in **Psalm 119:104-105** & **Psalm 119:130**, the author (God) is simply saying that the latter is the elucidation of the former. In this case, understanding, which is light, is what the Word of God brings.

When there is light, we are able to do things and take action. If we find ourselves not taking action or remaining in disobedience, it simply means that we lack understanding. For this reason, it is impossible to understand and not take action. What you do not know can simply be referred to as being in darkness on that matter. For instance, an engineer is enlightened in the field of engineering; but that same engineer can be in darkness in the field of accounting. This is what the devil preys on. He looks for those things that we are ignorant about and hits us hard. He did this to Eve in **Genesis 3**; hence the fall of human beings. This was and still is the only card the devil's got; unfortunately, it has remained effective through the ages, because of the carelessness and lack of understanding. A person without the knowledge and understanding of Jesus Christ as the savior is in darkness both physically and spiritually. This is because when we have the knowledge and understanding of Jesus as savior, and the dangers of living without Him, it will be absolutely impossible not to accept Him as Lord and savior.

So, if we keep increasing in our understanding (in God), we are increasing the brightness and intensity of our light in the spirit. We can be seen very clearly, and we become a terror and formidable opponent for the devil and his cohorts. We become a real threat to the kingdom of darkness; they know us by name and plan assaults at every opportunity to shut us down. We become a city that is set on a hill that cannot be hidden as per **Matthew 5:14**. The evil spirit in **Acts 19:15 NLT** (*But one time when they tried it, the evil spirit replied, "I know Jesus, and I know Paul, but who are you?"*) confirms this by mentioning Jesus and Paul on a first name basis. The next time you are attacked by the devil or his agents, remember it is because of your increasing level of understanding that is creating a light of high intensity in the spirit.

It is important to note that we are being attacked by the devil for two reasons. First, imagine if someone turns on the light when you are half-awake or half-asleep; most likely, you will construe the brightness of the light as a nuisance, because it would seem like it is going to damage your eyes. However, your eyes eventually adapt to this brightness because we are creatures of light. This is exactly how the devil feels when a child of God comes close to his operation. The same way the initial instinct will be to try to get rid of the light is exactly what the devil does with his assaults on us. Secondly, our understanding gives us an advantage over the devil. We can see him clearly and he cannot blindside us, as confirmed in **2 Corinthians 2:11 NLT** (*So, that Satan will not outsmart us. For we are familiar with his evil schemes*). This renders him so powerless, and that is something a prideful monster such as the devil doesn't like. In view of this, he looks for the slightest darkness (where we lack understanding) in us and attacks with deception. He does this to gain a sense of power and bring us down; however, with the right and continuous understanding in God, we will always be ahead and conquer him. Remember, Jesus, defeated him already (**Romans 8:37**).

Get Set: Understanding is Freedom

Freedom, as defined by Google, is *the power or right to act, speak, or think as one wants without hindrance or restraint.* Now, how is understanding freedom? Previously, we established that understanding simply connotes light. When you get it, you can proceed without any hindrance. Hence, we see it is understanding that gives the power or right to act, speak, or think as one wants without hindrance or restraint. Therefore, when we lack understanding we are not free; we are slaves of ignorance.

Furthermore, in **2 Corinthians 3:17 NLT** *(For the Lord is the Spirit, and wherever the **Spirit of the Lord is**, there is **freedom**)*, the Bible made us understand that freedom is synonymous with the Spirit of God (the Holy Spirit). This makes total sense because **John 16:13 NLT** tells us that, *"When the **Spirit of truth** comes, he will guide you into all truth. He will not speak on his own but will tell you what he has heard. He will tell you about the future."* This scripture established that the Holy Spirit is the Spirit of truth, and when you know the truth it will set you free (**John 8:32**). However, we know that nothing becomes true until we understand it. Yes, there are facts, but to reveal the truth out of these facts, understanding is needed. When we understand the facts, it becomes the truth to us. For example, experiments are performed to gain more understanding of theoretical (proven and unproven) facts. Once the experiments are concluded, we gain a better understanding and hence the undoubtable truth.

When facts are gathered, it is a norm to vet it, so that truth and falsehood are properly identified. Extensive efforts are usually made by legal practitioners via solicitation and investigation to validate facts and uncover the truth. However, the Holy Spirit, who is the Spirit of truth, can guide us into all truth if we let Him. This makes Him capable of setting us free; hence wherever He is, there is freedom. The truth that He carries and reveals makes His environment a place of freedom—where we are free to take action based on the understanding that He has made available.

Therefore, understanding is the freedom we need to live life to the fullest. And it is only the Spirit of God that can reveal this to us. You may say, "well, the understanding that I am looking for is not related to God." This might sound true, but ruminate on this: *"for through him (Jesus) God created everything in the heavenly realms and on earth. He made the things we can see and the things we can't see--such as thrones, kingdoms, rulers, and authorities in the unseen world. Everything was created through him and for him."* **Colossians 1:16 NLT, Emphasis added** and **James 1:17**: *"Whatever is good and perfect comes down to us from God our Father, who created all the lights in the heavens. He never changes or casts a shifting shadow."* We can see that regardless of what we are looking for, the answer and the truth can be found in and through God. He can guide us to the truth we desperately need.

In this day and age, God has delegated the revelation of

truth to the Spirit of truth (the Holy Spirit). Therefore, keeping Him out of anything is the best way to fail and remain in darkness. Engage Him in all things and your life will never remain the same. In the subsequent chapter, we'll discuss how to engage Him.

Go

We have established why understanding is so important; now, we are ready for the knowledge enveloped in this book. Also, it is very clear from all we've learned thus far that the Holy Spirit is needed for understanding. Could He also be the most important person of our time? Well, only time will tell eh! Anyways, the answer to this brooding question is explained in the pages of the subsequent chapters. I encourage you to get comfortable as we embark on this journey of getting to know the most important person today.

2

The Identity

There are many reasons people get into relationships, at a high level, the reasons are either genuine or mischievous. It is safe to say that most people get into relationships for their own benefit. But relationships can be essential or inessential. So, it is advisable to sustain useful relationships and sever useless relationships, to protect oneself from self-inflicted pain. There are other kinds of relationships that one will find themselves in, because they have no choice, like relationships with parents, siblings, family members and so on. Even though this is true, it is still our choice to either develop or abate meaningful relationships. I am not saying what to do, but just providing a statement of fact.

Our understanding of partners in a relationship and gains from a relationship will often determine if we want to develop it or not. The purpose of this chapter is to unveil the identity of the most important person and enhance our understanding of the importance of cultivating this relationship and taking it to the next level.

The Person

In any organization, the most important person is often the Chief Executive Officer or the Chairman (depending on the organization's structure). Ideally, the founder of an organization is its most important person; however, in some cases, they might no longer be an active part of the organization. In the case of a country or territory, the individual running the government or the head of state is the most important. As a matter of fact, anyone with or without a title, who runs the affairs of an entity or has the power to make changes that will directly or indirectly impact the lives of individuals is somewhat important.

There are no vacancies when it comes to power. There is always someone in charge. This is the law of nature; it is how we operate and function. Therefore, we can somewhat agree it is unreasonable to conclude that "there is no one behind the creation and sustainment of the earth and universe" (**Psalm 14:1**). In many countries laws, working for a group that plans to overthrow, deny or defy the existing government is considered treason. Treason simply means to be an adversary of the current government and hence the country, and as such, it is punishable by life imprisonment in Canada and death in the United States. Using this logic, we are citizens of the earth. Defying or denying the existence of the one in charge of the earth and universe will be construed as treason.

With that being said, the question becomes: Who is in charge of the earth? I bet this person is definitely important and should be known, do you agree with me? At this point, it is safe to say that the most important person of our time is the one in charge of the world we live in today; perhaps the one who founded it. The one who runs the affairs of the earth and universe, whose decisions have the ability to affect us, is the one we seek to know and build a relationship with. Human governments come and go; hence that can't be it.

As we will explore further in the subsequent chapter, having a relationship with people in power has its own advantages. We will have the opportunity to be heard where it matters, and it is definitely a good place to be.

In the scriptures below, we can see the Bible clearly confirms the identity of the most important person, and based on these definitions He is GOD. Though few different names were used to qualify Him (God, Lord and Most High), all these are simply pointing to the one and only true God.

Daniel 4:17b NLT, emphasis added — *so that everyone may know that the Most High (God) rules over the kingdoms of the world. He gives them to anyone he chooses--even to the lowliest of people.*

Romans 13:1b NLT —*For all authority comes from God, and those in positions of authority have been placed there by God.*

Psalm 103:19 NLT — *The LORD has made the heavens his throne; from there he rules over everything.*

Jeremiah 27:5 NLT, emphasis added — *With my great strength and powerful arm I (God) made the earth and all its people and every animal. I can give these things of mine to anyone I choose.*

Daniel 2:21 NLT, emphasis added — *He (God) controls the course of world events; he removes kings (and leaders) and sets up other kings (and leaders). He gives wisdom to the wise and knowledge to the scholars.*

The moment I referred to God, some were already turned

off. This is because you believe that you have issues with God. You think so because you don't know Him intimately or understand Him. Others know Him from afar; this could either mean knowing God via another person or what others have told them about Him. Evidently, it is only when we come closer to anything that we can get clearer details.

Though we have unveiled the identity as God, it is very important to continue by focusing more closely on God. This will help us understand who He is and how He is the most important. In my book "The Person You Should Know," I wrote about how many people jump to conclusions without any proper research. This is not just unwise, but absurd. They take their time to learn and discover other things, but when it comes to God, they shy away and come up with their own baseless conclusions—how sad. However, in this book, we will dig deep into God as needed. I advise we all approach the teachings of this book with an open mind; only then do we stand a chance of cultivating a good relationship with the most important person. Don't just stay far off and expect magic, God is not a magician but a miracle worker. Now, let's get to know God more.

The Person: God

As humans, we all have elements of our personalities that are unique to us. These attributes define us. Consequently, when an incident is described, we are quick in identifying the individual involved. This is possible because of our knowledge of the individual and their ways of doing things. The understanding of a person's personality is the beginning of a successful relationship. Many relationships, including marriages, end up in the gutter because a partner (or both of them) failed to understand the other's character. When this happens and resolution is unreachable, separation is inevitable. Notwithstanding, it is possible to get along with anybody if an individual wants to. This is why the Bible says in **Romans 12:18 NLT,** *do all that you can to live in peace with everyone.* As long as we understand their personality and we are willing to make it work, getting along is achievable. Thus, we are able to work with all kinds of people at our workplaces.

Just like us, God is also a being with characteristics and qualities distinctive to Him. In fact, according to **Genesis 1:27 NLT** (*So God created human beings in his own image. In the image of God, he created them; male and female he created them*), God made us in His image. And as such, some of the personalities of God are inherent in us. Therefore, we can see some similarities of God in us. This was why we were called gods in **Psalm 82:6 NLT** (*I say, 'You are gods; you are all children of the Most High.*) and Jesus reaffirmed it in **John 10:34 NLT** (*Jesus replied, "It is written in your own Scriptures that God said to certain leaders of the people, 'I say, you are gods!'"*). This is not heresy; it is the word of God.

In my book "The Person You Should Know," I thoroughly explained our nature within the context of its similarity to that of God. I encourage you to take some time to read it; it will help your understanding and reinforce some of the information in this book.

However, for the sake of our discussion here, I will quickly explain some of the similarities of our nature to God's nature.

Before God made us, God had spoken about it with another being.

Genesis 1:26 NLT, emphasis added — *Then God said, "**Let us** make human beings **in our image, to be like us**. (Because we reign over all things), They will reign over the fish in the sea, the birds in the sky, the livestock, all the wild animals on the earth, and the small animals that scurry along the ground.".*

The core of their conversation (i.e., *let us...in our image, to be like us*) is indicative that these other Beings are in the same calibre as God. Therefore, their product (i.e., human beings) will have a similar nature to God together with the other Beings. Consequently, like God, humans are triune in nature. As many anointed vessels of God have put it, "we are a **spirit** being, living in a **body** and we have a **soul**." Hence, we are in the form of a spirit, soul and body.

From the explanation above, we can say that the nature of God is triune. Perhaps, it is no coincidence that His name only has three letters—GOD. Now, let's prove that God is triune in nature like us. According to **2 Corinthians 13:14 NLT, emphasis added**, the Bible tells us, *"May the grace of the **Lord Jesus Christ**, the love of **God (the Father)**, and the fellowship of the **Holy Spirit** be with you all."* The nature revealed to us are God (the Father), God (the Son—Jesus Christ) and God (the Holy Spirit).

Since we know that spirit, soul and body are the compositions of human beings, likewise, Father, Son and Holy Spirit are the compositions of God. It is imperative to state that the same way the composition of humans carries distinctive identities, so also does God's. All of God's beings (the Father, Son and Holy Spirit) are God. And none of God's beings are lesser than the other. The combination of God's beings is simply called God. And the individuality of these beings is still God. I understand this might be too deep, but remember we are talking about the all-powerful God. Please follow the explanation, and I pray that God will give understanding in Jesus' name. Amen.

Like our nature, these beings are all connected. However, unlike our nature, each of God's beings has the ability and capacity to exist independently and function differently; hence the possibility of a trialogue in **Genesis 1:26**. Due to these facts, the three beings of God can work together or separately.

Each of these beings, like our own being (spirit, soul and body), has different primary functions. However, this does not in any way limit them. Remember, each being is God on His own and has all the power and authority of God. This is a deep and interesting topic; however, we must understand God's nature and the reason He decided to reveal Himself in such a way. We will explore each of these beings further in the preceding sections.

God: The Father

The Father is the primary existence of God; that is, He is the principal head of the Beings. Though the other two beings can operate and function on their own, each of them still depends on the Father.

John 5:30 NLT emphasis added — *I (Jesus) can do nothing on my own. I judge as God—the Father tells me. Therefore, my judgment is just, because I carry out the will of the one—the Father who sent me, not my own will.*

John 16:13 NLT emphasis added — *When the Spirit of truth comes, He will guide you into all truth. He will not speak on His own but will tell you what He has heard—from the Father. He will tell you about the future.*

This logic is reasonable because only one person can drive a car at any given time. Hence the Father is the head of the three coexisting beings of God known to us; this is why the other two members of God's nature are accountable to Him.

The Father is the core, foundation, and complete embodiment of God; you can also say the Father is the trunk of the God tree. Everything that God is can be found in this representation of God. You might wonder if the Father is the complete embodiment of God, why then do we have the other two representations of God? We will discuss this soon.

Knowing the Father and having a relationship with Him is the goal; this is why Jesus, during His lifetime on earth, always pointed to the Father. And the Holy Spirit, in this dispensation, will always refer us to the Father. Therefore, we pray to the Father, using the name of the Son (Jesus) (**John 16:23**) and by the help of the Holy Spirit (**Romans 8:26**). Hence the two representations of God (the Son and the Holy Spirit) will always refer us back to the Father and prepare us to know and get closer to the Father.

Let us use an analogy to expatiate further. In every organization, there is always the main person; often referred to as the Chief Executive Officer (CEO)—the most important person. Before anyone can visit the CEO, there are individuals that must be met and protocols that must be followed. These individuals make sure that the meeting with the CEO is productive for all parties involved, especially the CEO. They examine people who want to meet the CEO and the purpose of the meeting; if their reasons are cogent, they are prepared accordingly to meet the CEO. We refer to such people as executive assistance, receptionists and so on. This is similar but slightly different from God's protocol. God (the Father) can be likened to a CEO who has two executive assistants (Jesus and the Holy Spirit). These executive assistants are available to help us with the process of getting close to the Father. Unlike the organization structure I explained, these executive assistants do not turn away any person who wants to know the Father. Despite the fact that some people come with a sinister agenda (**Acts 8:9-24**), Jesus and the Holy Spirit continuously strive to give all a taste of what a relationship with the Father will be like. Hence the instruction of Jesus in **Mark 16:15 NLT**: *And then he told them, "Go into all the world and preach the Good News to **everyone**."* This is so because according to **Psalm 34:8**, all that is needed is a taste of God through His executive assistants.

Psalm 34:8 NLT — *Taste and see that the LORD is good. Oh, the joys of those who take refuge in him!*

I understand that I might be making this sound so simple, that is because it is simple. Though, there is more to the nature of God; but for now, we will just highlight some essentials. However, as we proceed further in knowing more about the Father, we will understand more about His nature. We will also learn about the other two beings and what they do to facilitate the process of knowing God the Father.

The Father is the head of God's nature and the architect of all creation (**Psalm 146:6**); hence He takes on the responsibilities associated with this position. These responsibilities often dictate His actions and reactions. We will explore this further.

The Father's Responsibilities
May the grace of the Lord Jesus Christ, the love of God (the Father), and the fellowship of the Holy Spirit be with you all. **(2 Corinthians 13:14 NLT)**

The scripture above listed the three Beings and what they offer. This scripture is a deep revelation of what you can rightly expect from each of these Beings. As it can be seen, each of these Being is associated with an attribute, and this is what drives their responsibilities. As we proceed, we will drill down through these attributes, but for now, let us hone in on that of the Father.

"The love of God (the Father)"—Love was used to portray the Father here. This is interesting because the old testament of the Bible has been regarded as the book of horror stories by some people. Their myopic perspective of the old testament has been the basis of their decision not to have a relationship with God. It is imperative to state that their perspective is inconsistent with the attribute of love that portrays the Father.

Yes, the old testament was indeed the dispensation of the Father. God created all things including time. Therefore, it can be rightly assumed that God doesn't joke around with time. He's got a timetable of all things.

1 Corinthians 14:33 NLT— *For God is not a God of disorder but of peace, as in all the meetings of God's holy people.*

For every act of God, there is timing linked to it. Like the popular saying *"God's time is the best."* This means that God has the right time for all things. The same is applicable here.

The earth has been in existence for over 4 Billion years. In all these years of earth's existence, there have been various dispensations. Things have been done differently across dispensations, but it is always consistent with the culture of the dispensation. It is only God that has the timetable for all eras of earth's existence. As part of God's plan, there will always be a "Being of God" in every dispensation of earth's existence. So, Jesus said, *"I will not leave you orphans"*. (**John 14:18**). This has remained valid across all eras on the earth, in which the primary Being of God is always known to the people of that time. Hence my statement that God the Father was the primary Being the God in the dispensation of the old testament.

In the old testament, there were only a few manifestations of the Holy Spirit and allusions to Jesus; only God the Father was explicitly known in that dispensation. The God of an age can always come in contact with the people of that age. As recorded, the old testament was the time of ancient Israelites; the God that the people encountered most times was neither the Holy Spirit nor Jesus, it was the Father. And with only three representations of God known to us, the only conclusion from the records of the Bible is that the God of that age was God—the Father.

From **2 Corinthians 13:14**, it is apparent that the responsibility of the Father is to love us. This is quite simple but may seem untrue or impossible, especially when one is fixated on the old testament and the evil in the world today.

1 John 4:16 NLT — We know how much God loves us, and we have put our trust in his love. God is love, and all who live in love live in God, and God lives in them

Do you know that it is the love of God that led Him to

release His other Beings (Jesus and the Holy Spirit)? We will explore this soon. But first, if the God of the Old Testament is the Father, why are there so many unloving acts portrayed by the God who is Love?

The Old Testament Horror Stories

Over the years, we may have heard preachers call the Bible God's love letter to humanity. However, when we take a glance at the old testament, most of the stories contradict this notion. Also, the affirmation earlier that God—the Father—is the God of the old testament contradicts the notion that His nature and responsibility is love. Is this an instance the Bible contradicts itself? No, and this is why.

The love of God is for all His creation. However, not all of God's creation enjoys the love of God. The reason for this is because, even though the love of God is equal to all, how we respond to or accept His love is the determinant of the kind of grace we carry and experience. Hence why it seems as though some are loved by God more than others. To prove this point, despite the fact that some people blatantly rejected God, He did not close the gate of heaven from releasing their basic needs of life. This is proof of God's equal love for all.

Matthew 5:45 NLT — *In that way, you will be acting as true children of your Father in heaven. For he gives his sunlight to both the evil and the good, and he sends rain on the just and the unjust alike.*

In some countries, there are general benefits for its populace; for example, Canadians can consult with a physician at no cost. However, within these countries, some of its citizens have access to more benefits that are unavailable to the populace; for example, by virtue of working for some employers, some Canadians have access to prescription and dental services for little or no cost. This is not discrimination; it is rather an entitlement for working in such an organization and residing in Canada. Likewise, if a person accepts to be in a relationship with God, you should expect them to experience a different kind of grace than the general public.

What I have just explained is the foundation of God's love towards us. His love is unconditional. But our acceptance of this love puts us under the grace that makes us His priority.

Zachariah 2:8b NKJV — *for he who touches you touches the apple of His eye.*

The children of ancient Israel became the beloved and the favorite of God because their ancestor (Abraham) accepted the call of God by being obedient (**Genesis 12**). We do not know how many people God had spoken to before and after Abraham. God may have called another person simultaneously with Abraham. However, what is apparent is that Abraham accepted God's call. Consequently, this made him and his descendants recipients of God's abundant grace and precedence, which is still evident today.

Furthermore, among the children of Israel, we saw this principle at play again. Moses made a call in the camp of the Israelites, for those committed to God to publicly signify their stance. The Levites were the only ones that answered Moses' call because they genuinely supported God. Consequently, it is not a surprise that God chose them and set them apart from the others.

Exodus 32:26 NLT, emphasis added —*So, he (Moses) stood at the entrance to the camp and shouted, "All of you who are on the LORD's side, come here and join me." And all the **Levites** gathered around him.*

Numbers 3:12 NLT — *"Look, I have chosen the **Levites** from among the **Israelites** to serve as substitutes for all the firstborn sons of the people of Israel. The Levites belong to me.*

Therefore, we have the power to determine our destinies, when it pertains to the realm we operate in with God.

The other point to mention is the code of conduct outlined by God, the Father, in the old testament. Honestly, some of those laws were synonymous with that age. But from our little experience, we know that the human level of understanding does evolve, but God does not change (**Malachi 3:6**). Our evolution in our understanding is what determines the level at which God deals with us. I am not in any way saying that the law of God has changed—definitely not. Oftentimes, because of the flaw in our understanding, it seems as though it changes. However, our understanding of His love evolves as well. For example, the ten commandments were given by God Himself (**Exodus 31**); however, the essence of these commandments was love.

Mark 12:31 NLT — *The second is equally important: 'Love your neighbor as yourself.' No other commandment is greater than these.*

Romans 13:8-10 NLT — *Owe nothing to anyone—except for your obligation to love one another. If you love your neighbor, you will fulfill the requirements of God's law. For the commandments say, "You must not commit adultery. You must not murder. You must not steal. You must not covet." These—and other such commandments—are summed up in this one commandment: "Love your* neighbor as yourself." Love does no wrong to others, so love fulfills the requirements of God's law.

During the era of the ten commandments, humans were incapable of understanding this kind of love. So, God had to give the law, in accordance with the culture and understanding of that time. When humans evolved in their understanding, insight was gained from God's word that the same law (given in times past) can be fulfilled through love. Hence it is humans' understanding that drives their interpretation of God; this is why the Bible says in **Romans 3:4 NLT**, *"Of course not! Even if everyone else is a liar, God is true. As the Scriptures say about him, "You will be proved right in what you say, and you will win your case in court."*

God: The Son—Jesus

As established earlier, Jesus is one of the Beings that can be deemed as one of the Father's executive assistants. Jesus is the only form of God that appeared and lived as a man on the earth. He was born many years ago as a fulfilment of prophecies, as confirmed by history. The reason for Jesus is quite simple.

Matthew 1:21 NLT — *And she will have a son, and you are to name him Jesus, for he will save his people from their sins.*

But what is sin? and why do people need to be saved from sin?

God's intention when He made us was to have a close relationship and rapport with us. Hence God came to visit His creation in the garden when the cool evening breeze was blowing.

Genesis 3:8 NLT — *When the cool evening breezes were blowing, the man and his wife heard the LORD God walking about in the garden. So, they hid from the LORD God among the trees.*

But when Adam and Eve (whom I will start to refer to as the first people) disobeyed God's command, that is, sinned (**Genesis 3**), they were not just cast out of the garden, but also from the presence of God. Therefore, sin is simply to disobey the command of God. The first people lost the relationship and rapport they once had with God, the Father, as a consequence of their sin. This was not because the Father was mean, but because *"God is pure and cannot stand the sight of evil—sin"* (**Habakkuk 1:13** emphasis added). It was from here that we all became sinners; this is because like begets like. Since sin is evil, the first people were cast out of the Father's presence. We couldn't approach God's presence, because we were all evil by genetics (**Romans 3:23**).

From scripture, we know that it was the breath of God that made us a living soul. Therefore, we cannot be alive without the breath of God. As such, the breath of God in us longs for God; hence we will always have a void in us that yearns for God, all the days of our lives.

Genesis 2:7 NLT — *Then the LORD God formed the man from the dust of the ground. He breathed the breath of life into the man's nostrils, and the man became a living person.*

The sad thing is that many people try various things to fill this void. It is the quest to fill the human void that the devil has exploited over the years. He has created an alternative—idols—to deceive and put a leash on humans. Many of us who are gullible and lack understanding have fallen into this trap many times over, and even today. The devil has perfected this charade, by making it convincingly real to his victims. They believe they are on the right path, when in fact it is nothing but a farce (**Proverbs 14:12**).

Jesus said there is no other way to God—the Father—except through Him. How do I know that Jesus' assertion is accurate? Authentic history books substantiate Jesus' existence, death and resurrection. Therefore, there is absolutely no need to doubt Jesus' statements and acts in the Bible.

John 14:16 NLT — *Jesus told him, "I am the way, the truth, and the life. No one can come to the Father except through me.*

Based on the Bible and historical facts, it is safe to say the following. Anyway, that does not specify the necessity for believing in Jesus Christ will always lead to a false god—not the one true God.

Proverbs 14:12 NLT — *There is a path before each person that seems right, but it ends in death.*

You may say, I have been in a non-Christian religion since birth, and I have also seen various acts and miracles; it is irrefutable that my religion is a way to the one true God. Let me shock you, ***IT IS NOT!*** There are no alternative ways to God outside Jesus Christ. Every legitimate company has the way they recruit; any other way not specified by the company is deemed fraudulent. If there was or will be any other way to God, the Father, it would have been prophesied or Jesus would have made mention of it. However, all prophecies pointed to only Jesus Christ, even before His birth. To surprise you further, any form of Christianity without an emphasis on receiving Jesus to be saved is a fallacy. Miracles that emanate from sources outside Jesus are counterfeit and another fulfillment of the scripture—**2 Corinthians 11:14**.

2 Corinthians 11:14 NLT — *But I am not surprised! Even Satan disguises himself as an angel of light.*

No one in their right mind will follow the path of darkness into destruction. This is why deception remains a lethal weapon in the hands of the devil, to lure people into the path of darkness.

The first people fell into sin because they accepted the lies and deceit of the devil. This culminated in their separation from God because the breath of God in them had been severed from its source. From then onwards, humans (including those unborn) have been separated from God, because we were all procreated from the first people. This separation is the actual reason for our feeling of emptiness and our need for the supernatural—God. Anyone who is not properly connected to the source of their life will always feel empty and have a void in them. How this void is filled really matters. If you fill it with anything other than the one true God, there will be chaos in your being. There are so many examples of this in this day and age.

Do not be deceived, you cannot fill the void created by the longing of the breath of God in you with something else and expect effective functioning; problems are guaranteed to compound in your life. Many people have attempted to fill the void in them with the wrong thing and ended up disappointed; this can also lead to suicide. On the other hand, some people have filled it with a counterfeit. Though it might appear similar to the real thing, it is fake. This is evidenced by the good in some areas of the individual's life and the problems in other areas. A classic example of this, are individuals that fill the void in them with their career. The commitment of these individuals could be yielding tremendous results in their careers; however, other areas of their lives, like marriage and family are in disarray. This is so because they only covered one aspect of the void. It is imperative to say that, there is no way to fill the void without the one true God.

When we connect the breath of God to the right source, we will have all-round success (**John 10:10**). The absence of all-round success in a person's life signifies a connection deficiency—to the right source. Therefore, it is our responsibility to examine ourselves and ensure we are connected to the right source.

The void created by the sin of the first people was the reason why God, the Father, sent Jesus. Hence the statement in **Matthew 1:21**. The purpose of Jesus is therefore to reconnect us to the right source of our breath—the Father. In so doing, fill the void/separation created by sin.

John 3:16-17 NLT, **emphasis added** — *For this is how God loved the world: He gave his one and only Son, so that everyone who believes in him will not perish but have eternal life. God sent his Son into the world not to judge the world, but to save the world—and fill the void through Him.*

The Son's Responsibilities

Earlier we learned that Jesus existed to fill the void created by sin, by reconnecting us to the Father. Therefore, His responsibility is based on this mandate and this we'll explore next. As always, the purpose is the foundation for responsibility. For example, a parent's purpose is to leave an inheritance for their children (**Proverbs 13:22**); hence it is their responsibility to save and invest for the future of their children.

The mandate of reconnecting us to the Father was the main reason Jesus came to the earth. Every other benefit that comes with knowing or encountering Jesus is just the icing on the cake. The sole purpose of Jesus' life, suffering, death and resurrection were to reconcile/reconnect us to God (**2 Corinthians 5**). Now, let us expatiate on each of these for better understanding and appreciation.

Jesus' Life

As per history, Jesus lived for about 33 years and a bit. During His lifetime, all He did was to teach about the Father and prepare us for the Holy Spirit (we will explore the Holy Spirit next). Jesus was so focused on the Father that everything He said led back to Him.

John 5:19 NLT — *So Jesus explained, "I tell you the truth, the Son can do nothing by himself. He does only what he sees the Father doing. Whatever the Father does, the Son also does.*

John 6:38 NLT, emphasis added — *For I have come down from heaven to do the will of God—The Father who sent me, not to do my own will.*

John 8:28 NLT — *So Jesus said, "When you have lifted up the Son of Man on the cross, then you will understand that I Am he. I do nothing on my own but say only what the Father taught me.*

John 12:49-50 NLT — *I don't speak on my own authority. The Father who sent me has commanded me what to say and how to say it. And I know his commands lead to eternal life; so, I say whatever the Father tells me to say.*

John 14:10 NLT — *Don't you believe that I am in the Father* *and the Father is in me? The words I speak are not my own, but my Father who lives in me does his work through me.*

As seen from the scriptures, it was clear that His life matched the responsibility set before Him. He taught us about the Father all through His life. This was His focus when He was on earth. I heard a statement some time ago; it was asked, "if homosexuality is against the will of God, how come Jesus never addressed it in His lifetime?" First off, yes, it is against the will of God, because this was one of the many sins that led to the destruction of Sodom and Gomorrah (**Genesis 18 and 19**). God's thoughts on this were pretty clear. Secondly, such a question is simply a display of a lack of understanding. Here is why. Jesus' purpose wasn't to tell us what is sin and what is not, that is the job of the Holy Spirit.

John 16:8 NLT — *And when he comes, he will convict the world of its sin, and of God's righteousness, and of the coming judgment.*

This was why the Pharisees tried at various times to trick Him into condemning or stating if something was a sin or not; however, He never fell into this trap. The job of Jesus at that time was to tell us about the Father. He was to create a portal that connects us back to the Father.

John 3:17 NLT, emphasis added — *God sent his Son—Jesus into the world not to judge the world, but to save the world through him.*

Matthew 5:17 NLT — *"Don't misunderstand why I have come. I did not come to abolish the law of Moses or the writings of the prophets. No, I came to accomplish their purpose.*

All the commandments of God still stand, because God does not change or evolve. In **Numbers 23:19 NLT**, we see that

THE MOST IMPORTANT PERSON OF OUR TIME - 33

God is not a man, so he does not lie. He is not human, so he does not change his mind. Has he ever spoken and failed to act? Has he ever promised and not carried it through?".

As part of Jesus's responsibilities, He made it easier for us to obey. He did this by taking our place

2 Corinthians 2:21 NLT — *For God made Christ, who never sinned, to be the offering for our sin, so that we could be made right with God through Christ.*

He also emphasizes just one law that trumps and automatically fulfills all the other laws if we obey.

Deuteronomy 6:5 NLT — *And you must love the LORD your God with all your heart, all your soul, and all your strength.*

Leviticus 19:18 NLT — *"Do not seek revenge or bear a grudge against a fellow Israelite, but love your neighbor as yourself. I am the LORD.*

Mark 12:30-31 NLT — *And you must love the Lord your God with all your heart, all your soul, all your mind, and all your strength.' The second is equally important: 'Love your neighbor as yourself.'' No other commandment is greater than these."*

Romans 13:8-10 NLT — *Owe nothing to anyone—except for your obligation to love one another. If you love your neighbor, you will fulfill the requirements of God's law. For the commandments say, "You must not commit adultery. You must not murder. You must not steal. You must not covet." These—and other such commandments—are summed up in this one commandment: "Love your neighbor as yourself." Love does no wrong to others, so love fulfills the requirements of God's law.*

His Suffering and Death

Do you know that Jesus did not need to suffer or die? The fact that He is the God of all, He is capable of getting everything He desires.

Matthew 26:53-54 NLT — *Don't you realize that I could ask my Father for thousands of angels to protect us, and he would send them instantly? But if I did, how would the Scriptures be fulfilled that describe what must happen now?*

However, if Jesus was going to attain His purpose, it was, therefore, His responsibility to suffer and die. Yes, it was our mess (from the first people) and primarily our responsibility to clean it up. But God, in His infinite mercy, sent Jesus to clean up our mess. He knew that we have tried so many times and failed woefully.

You may say well, He can still clean up the mess without having to die. Yes, you are right, but God is a God of integrity.

Matthew 5:37 ESV — *Let what you say be simply 'Yes' or 'No'; anything more than this comes from evil.*

Matthew 24:35 NLT — *Heaven and earth will disappear, but my words will never disappear.*

In fact, according to the law of Moses, nearly everything was purified with blood, because *without the shedding of blood, there is no forgiveness* (**Hebrews 9:22 NLT**). We can see that in accordance with God's ordinance, someone or something must suffer and die to pay for sin. This was the reason for sacrifices in the old testament. Hence Jesus was *pierced for our rebellion, crushed for our sin, beaten and whipped, so that we could be healed and made whole* (**Isaiah 53:5 NLT**). *Despite the fact that*

Jesus was rich, he became poor for our sakes, so that by His poverty He could make us rich (**2 Corinthians 8:9 NLT**).

In addition to the fact that His death is the payment for our sin, His death also made a way to the Father by silencing the devil and putting us in charge.

Matthew 28:18 NLT — *Jesus came and told his disciples; I have been given all authority in heaven and on earth.*

Jesus' statement in **Matthew 28:18** was after His resurrection from death. This could only mean that after He had descended into the grave and paid the price for our sin, He challenged the devil and won. Hence His claim to the power.

During one of Jesus' temptations in the wilderness, the devil said, *"I will give it all to you, if you will kneel down and worship me"* (**Matthew 4:9 NLT**). This can only mean that the earthly things (**Matthew 4:8**) the devil was offering belonged to him before Jesus died. When the devil made those statements, Jesus didn't argue with the devil or refute it, because it was valid. The first people had dominion (**Genesis 1:28**); when they fell, they ceded their dominion to the devil (**Luke 4:6**). However, when Jesus died, He retrieved dominion from the devil and gave it back to us. Therefore, *"whatever you forbid on earth will be forbidden in heaven, and whatever you permit on earth will be permitted in heaven"* (**Matthew 18:18 NLT**). Glory to God!

We see again that the purpose of His suffering and death was to reconnect us with God and give us all-round success as promised.

His Resurrection

Jesus' death and resurrection were among many things He alluded to His disciples when He was here on earth. There were also prophecies about His death and resurrection.

Mark 9:31 NLT — *For he wanted to spend more time with his disciples and teach them. He said to them, "The Son of Man is going to be betrayed into the hands of his enemies. He will be killed, but three days later he will rise from the dead.*

Luke 18:31-33 NLT — *Taking the twelve disciples aside, Jesus said, "Listen, we're going up to Jerusalem, where all the predictions of the prophets concerning the Son of Man will come true. He will be handed over to the Romans, and he will be mocked, treated shamefully, and spit upon. They will flog him with a whip and kill him, but on the third day he will rise again."*

If Jesus' statements and the prophecies about His death and resurrection were false, then *all our preaching and faith is futile* (**1 Corinthians 15:14 NLT**). However, we know that they all came to pass (**Romans 8:34**); hence His promise of coming back (**John 14:2-3**) and His promises of our all-round success will definitely come to pass.

Habakkuk 2:3 NLT — *This vision is for a future time. It describes the end, and it will be fulfilled. If it seems slow in coming, wait patiently, for it will surely take place. It will not be delayed.*

1 John 5:13-15 NLT — *I have written this to you who believe in the name of the Son of God, so that you may know you have eternal life. And we are confident that he hears us whenever we ask for anything that pleases him. And since we know he hears us when we make our requests, we also know that he will give us what we ask for.*

Furthermore, the resurrection of Jesus distinguishes Him and proves that He is the one true God and the only way to the Father. Every other prophet and leader of religion has come and died; neither Mohammed nor Buddha resurrected after their death. This is because only the true God can defeat death.

1 Corinthians 15:55-57 NLT — *"O death, where is your victory? O death, where is your sting?" For sin is the sting that results in death, and the law gives sin its power. But thank God! He gives us victory over sin and death through our Lord Jesus Christ.*

Jesus' triumph over death validated His power over death and sin. It takes the sinless God to save sinful people (**1 Corinthians 5:21** & **2 Corinthians 15:21**). According to **1 Corinthians 15:55-57**, only Jesus has power over death; this was why every other prophet and leader of religion could not resurrect as Jesus did when they died. Therefore, every religion without Jesus (as the Lord and savior) is not leading to the one true God.

As mentioned earlier in this chapter, the love of God is the same for all; however, how we receive this love is what determines the kind of grace we operate under. By accepting Jesus as Lord and Savior, we are exposed to the full dose of the love of God. This is because Jesus opens us to the grace that makes us God's first priority. This was the reason for the statement in **2 Corinthians 13:14** NLT, *"May the grace of the Lord Jesus Christ."* It was Jesus' responsibility to create the path for us to receive the love of God, by making sure that we know the Father. Operating in this grace makes us God's priority and grants us entry to heaven at the end of our days on earth.

God: The Holy Spirit

As the name implies, the Holy Spirit is a spirit being. He is the other being that makes up the Godhead. The Holy Spirit is the Spirit of God, which makes Him God. As we have learned earlier, He can also be deemed as executive assistance in God's quest to restore our relationship with Him.

The Holy Spirit has always been in existence (**Genesis 1:2 and Luke 3:22**). Unlike Jesus, He was never born, neither did He die; hence He did not resurrect. He relates with us from within. Since He is Spirit, He often relates with our spirit. Unlike Jesus, who related with us from the outside during His lifetime on earth.

Let's not forget that the Father's goal is for us to be reconnected to the source of our breath—the Father (**Genesis 2:7**). Jesus came to reveal the Father to us and create the avenue/door/portal (**John 10:9 and John 14:6**) that connects us to the Father. The Holy Spirit maintains this avenue and keeps us connected to the Father throughout our lifetime. Think of it this way, we come to God through Jesus. But remain in God via the Holy Spirit (**Ephesians 1:13**).

John 10:9 NLT, emphasis added — *Yes, I am the gate (door). Those who come in through me will be saved. They will come and go freely and will find good pastures.*

John 14:6 NLT — *I am the way, the truth, and the life. No one can come to the Father except through me.*

Everything that is worth something requires maintenance. Due to the nature of Jesus' mission, He had to come in the form of a man; as such He could not live forever. This was why when Jesus was preparing His disciple for His departure, He told them, *"But in fact, it is best for you that I go away, because if I don't, the Advocate won't come. If I do go away, then I will send him to you"* (**John 16:7 NLT**). The fact is that there are so many distractions and weaknesses in our nature. As such, we need someone who is superior to continually guide and direct us. If Jesus had left without handing us over to another God Being, His work on the cross would have been futile. Jesus' work has continued saving countless lives because it is being maintained by the Holy Spirit. The power of the work on the cross is as potent as ever, due to the majestic handling of God–the Holy Spirit. Yes, the work is futile in some people's lives, because of the deception of the devil. But Jesus' work remains potent in more lives, because of the power of God–the Holy Spirit.

The mission of the Holy Spirit is quite simple. Jesus is the door that we come through. Within the enclosure of this door is a staircase that leads to the Father; this staircase is the Holy Spirit. One step at a time, He is helping us, grooming us, teaching us, counselling us and shaping us into the best we are destined to be. He is doing this to prepare us to meet the Father as a perfect bride when we are done here on earth. Remember, the main obstacle in our relationship with God is the sin nature that we inherited from the first people. God cannot stand impurity; it is therefore the work of the Holy Spirit to make sure we are perfect (sinless) when we meet God the Father.

Ephesians 5:25-27 NLT, emphasis added — *For husbands, this means love your wives, just as Christ loved the church. He gave up his life for her to make her holy and clean, washed by the cleansing of God's word. He did this to present her to himself as a glorious* *church without a spot or wrinkle or any other blemish. Instead, she will be holy and without fault.*

Therefore, the work of Jesus opens the door for the work of the Holy Spirit. Jesus' sacrifice created the way to salvation and the Holy Spirit sustains this way. The Holy Spirit is the last line of defence before we meet the Father. Therefore, the work of the Holy Spirit is continuous, until we leave the earth through physical death or rapture.

Fellowship

...and the fellowship of the Holy Spirit be with you all (**2 Corinthians 13:14 NLT**).

Part of the reason for the existence of the Holy Spirit is rooted in the scripture above. As established earlier, the Holy Spirit is to guide us until we meet the Father. We cannot meet the Father in heaven until we are done here on earth. Therefore, while we are here on earth, we are to relate with the Holy Spirit the most. This relationship is what the Bible referred to as *"fellowship."*

Fellowship simply means to commune. Our fellowship with the Holy Spirit is what gives us access to the heart of the Father. Did you ask how? The heart of the Father is where the will of the Father is stored. Access to this will give us the ability to always please the Father and grow our relationship with Him. However, we are not yet perfect to have that kind of access.

Romans 3:23 NLT, emphasis added — *For everyone has sinned; we all fall short of God's (the Father's) glorious standard.*

This is why we cannot see the heart of the Father directly. Our sinful nature deters us from doing so, hence we need a medium and that is what fellowship with God's Spirit provides. When we get to heaven, we will be in the presence of God, the Father with no intermediaries between us. Until then, we need both Jesus and the Holy Spirit more than anything. Therefore, it is safe to say that when we get to heaven, we will be perfect. But for now, we can only know the heart of the Father (which is needed to build our relationship with Him) through His Spirit.

1 Corinthians 2:11 NLT — *No one can know a person's thoughts except that person's own spirit, and no one can know God's thoughts except God's own Spirit.*

Fellowship is, therefore, a very important necessity today. A person without the Holy Spirit is like a body without life. In the same way, *"having the easy way but taking the hardest way,"* perfectly describes a Christian without the Holy Spirit, that is those that never engage Him through fellowship.

The Holy Spirit's Responsibilities

The responsibilities of the Holy Spirit are very broad, due to the nature of tasks He undertakes. Some of these include sustaining the way created by Jesus, enabling us to maintain our salvation and perfecting us to meet the Father.

In reality, it is simply impossible to list out all the responsibilities of the Holy Spirit. However, I will talk about a few of them to facilitate insight. Let's go by His names.

The Holy Spirit

As His name implies, He is Holy. **Hebrews 12:14 NLT** tells us to *"Work at living in peace with everyone, and work at living a* *holy life, for those who are not holy will not see the Lord.* So, holiness is a requirement to see God; but if we disobey God, we will never see Him (**1 John 2:3**). Therefore, holiness is obeying God; to simply do whatever God asks us to do.

We can see God in two ways. The first way is during our lifetime on earth; we can see Him through His acts and essence. The second way is in heaven—after our life on earth. Seeing God on earth and in heaven is rooted in holiness. It is the responsibility of the Holy Spirit to ensure we see God on earth and in heaven. He does this by convicting us of our sin (**John 16:8**).

John 16:8 NLT — *And when he comes, he will convict the world of its sin, and of God's righteousness, and of the coming judgment.*

Notice how the scripture used the word "*convict*" rather than "*condemn*." This is very important because these two words are significantly different in meaning. Conviction is to facilitate repentance and restoration (i.e., turning back to God), while condemnation is to dehumanize and destroy a person's relationship with God. The purpose of conviction is for us to genuinely repent of our sins and never intentionally do it again; hence making us holy in the process. When we cautiously strive to refrain from a life of sin, we are striving to obey God; at its core, this is holiness. I say striving because there are times that we may fall (**Proverbs 24:16**). But even when we fall, we can be holy again once we repent. This is so because the moment we repent genuinely, we just obey God and as such we are holy again (**1 John 1:9**). The focus is not on how many times we sin or not sin, but rather our love for God and our desire to please Him. If this is our driving force, we will always stay holy with the help of the Holy Spirit.

The Spirit of Truth and Freedom

When the Spirit of truth comes, he will guide you into all truth. He will not speak on his own but will tell you what he has heard. He will tell you about the future. (**John 16:13 NLT**)

The Spirit of truth means the spirit that lets us know what is true and what is not. In **John 8:32 NLT** *(And you will know the truth, and the truth will set you free)*, we see that freedom is a virtue that comes with the truth. I define "Truth" as the revelation of the word of God (**John 17:17**). When revelation is released, light comes. In **Psalm 119:130 NLT** *(The entrance of Your words gives light; It gives understanding to the simple)*, the Psalmist confirms the fact that the word of God brings light. This it does, by giving understanding. Revelation simply means to understand, to see and to comprehend; this is what the Holy Spirit gives. Whatever we understand becomes true to us; nothing becomes true until it is understood.

Psalm 119:105 NLT — *Your commandments give me understanding; no wonder I hate every false way of life. Your word is a lamp to guide my feet and a light for my path.*

When understanding comes, illumination/light is released to guide our metaphorical feet. We are ushered into action that will lead to our freedom by the instructions of His Word. Hence it is impossible to have revelation/understand and disobey. Therefore, in the truth that is revealed by the Holy Spirit lies our deliverance and freedom. Consequently, the truth we require to be who God has destined us to be can only be revealed to us by the Holy Spirit.

From the scriptures, it is clear that freedom accompanies truth. Therefore, the Holy Spirit is both the Spirit of freedom and the Spirit of truth. The truth that He reveals is what makes His presence an atmosphere of freedom. His truth is what sets us free from lies, bondages and deception of the devil.

2 Corinthians 3:17 NLT — *For the Lord is the Spirit, and wherever the Spirit of the Lord is, there is freedom.*

The Spirit of Power

But you will receive power when the Holy Spirit comes upon you. And you will be my witnesses, telling people about me everywhere-in Jerusalem, throughout Judea, in Samaria, and to the ends of the earth." **(Acts 1:8 NLT)**

To survive in this world we live in, both spiritual and physical powers are needed. However, spiritual power is more important than physical power. This is so because the spiritual controls the physical. Everything that appears in the physical was done and sealed prior in the spiritual. Job's calamity was sealed in the spiritual before its manifestation in the physical (**Job 1:12**).

For example, since Jesus is God, this means He already existed before He was born in the physical. To prove this point, let's look at an incident in the book of Daniel.

Daniel 3:25 NKJV — *Look!" he answered, "I see four men loose, walking in the midst of the fire; and they are not hurt, and the form of the fourth is like the Son of God.*

Nebuchadnezzar saw the son of God not a son of God. There is a difference and here it is. Jesus is the son of God and we believers are one of God's sons and daughters. So, I am a son, you are a son, but Jesus is the Son.

Romans 8:29 NLT, emphasis added — *For God knew his people in advance, and he chose them to become like His Son, so that His Son-Jesus would be the firstborn among many brothers and sisters.*

Ephesians 1:5 NLT —*God decided in advance to adopt us into his own family by bringing us to himself through Jesus Christ. This is what he wanted to do, and it gave him great pleasure.*

John 3:16 NKJV — *For God so loved the world that He gave His only begotten Son, that whoever believes in Him should not perish but have everlasting life.*

We are God's adopted children, but Jesus is the only begotten Son of God. The Bible said Nebuchadnezzar saw *"the Son of God"*—Jesus. However, this happened long before Jesus was even born in the physical. There are other biblical references that validate that Jesus is the Son of God.

Mark 5:7 NLT — *With a shriek, he screamed, "Why are you interfering with me, Jesus, Son of the Highest God? In the name of God, I beg you, don't torture me!"*

Matthew 3:17 NLT — *And a voice from heaven said, "This is my dearly loved Son, who brings me great joy."*

In **Mark 5:7**, the demons confirmed that Jesus was the son of God. God also confirmed that Jesus was His son in **Matthew 3:17**, during His baptism. In **Jeremiah 1:5 NLT**, God said to Jeremiah, *"I knew you before I formed you in your mother's womb. Before you were born, I set you apart and appointed you as my prophet to the nations."* How else could God have known

Jeremiah? It can only be because Jeremiah's spirit existed in God spiritually before He was knitted together by God in His mother's womb **(Psalm 139:13)** and born physically.

Due to the superiority of the spiritual, those with spiritual power are always above those without spiritual power, even in the physical realm. This is why some people get involved in all sorts of diabolical power to stay on top. But just like every valuable thing, all of these diabolical powers often come at a price. Many have used unthinkable things such as a part of themselves, a close relative, even children and other people's destinies in exchange for diabolical power. A person without spiritual power is simply at the mercy of those with spiritual power.

As children of God, the Holy Spirit gives us the power that keeps us afloat. Therefore, *we are not at the mercy of anyone, but all things are at our mercy.* Glory to God!

Matthew 18:18 NLT — *I tell you the truth, whatever you forbid on earth will be forbidden in heaven, and whatever you permit on earth will be permitted in heaven.*

We can decide and declare what happens and we can face all the challenges of life with boldness. Jesus claimed all the power and the Holy Spirit simply makes this power available to us at all times.

Matthew 28:18 NLT — *Jesus came and told his disciples, "I have been given all authority in heaven and on earth."*

If we belong to Jesus, we have this power at our disposal any day and any time. Therefore, do not be intimidated by the devil because he is under your feet. *We have been given authority over all the power of the enemy, and we can walk among snakes and scorpions and crush them, and nothing will injure us* **(Luke**

10:19 NLT). Glory to God! All we have to do is build a good rapport with the Holy Spirit; in so doing, we can use His power as often as we need it to the glory of God.

The Spirit of Help

And the Holy Spirit helps us in our weakness. For example, we don't know what God wants us to pray for. But the Holy Spirit prays for us with groanings that cannot be expressed in words. (**Romans 8:26 NLT**)

The Holy Spirit helps us in so many things. The Bible made us understand in **James 4:3 NLT** *(And even when you ask, you don't get it because your motives are all wrong—you want only what will give you pleasure)* that when we pray without the help of the Holy Spirit, our prayer will not be answered. This is because we are either asking wrongly or with the wrong motives. The Holy Spirit helps us to ask the right things; He will even pray with us if we let Him. Yes, Google has answers, but the way we search determines what we get. I have heard someone say to me, "It's not about how hard you work that produces results; it is how smart." This is true, the various things we do can be done stress-free through the help of the Holy Spirit.

The concept of praying in the Spirit in **Ephesians 6:18 NLT** *(Pray in the Spirit at all times and on every occasion. Stay alert and be persistent in your prayers for all believers everywhere)* is to help us utilize the ever-present help of the Holy Spirit. Praying in the Spirit simply means yielding to the Holy Spirit, who then prays through us in His own way (this may include His language and His own terms). Remember, Jesus is our intercessor in Heaven (**Romans 8:34**) and the Holy Spirit is our intercessor on earth (**Romans 8:26**). We should let Him intercede for us through us.

Let us not forget that the Spirit is also God and therefore knows all things (yes, including your schooling and work). Praying and/or doing anything without help is not wise. If you are getting some results "without Him", imagine the greater and stress-free results you stand to get with Him.

As a child of God, if there is any weakness you are struggling with, involving the Holy Spirit is your only way out. We don't need to do it in our power anymore, because it is a part of the Holy Spirit's responsibility. Let us tap into the abundance of the Holy Spirit to make our life better.

Finally, a servant of God once said, *"any faith that puts all the responsibility on God is fake."* This is particularly true here. The Holy Spirit is there to help us. But we still have to do our part and He will help us. For example, He helps us to pray. However, it is still our responsibility to open our mouth; when we do so, He will fill it with the right words and the right language.

Luke 12:11-12 NLT — *And when you are brought to trial in the synagogues and before rulers and authorities, don't worry about how to defend yourself or what to say, for the Holy Spirit will teach you at that time what needs to be said.*

As we can see in the scripture above, the Holy Spirit will inspire, but the individual will still have to do the speaking. This is the way the Holy Spirit helps. He trains us to be warriors and not weaklings. Therefore, entreat His help and be willing to do your part.

3

Who is the God of this Age?

Previously, we've established that there is a Being of God in every dispensation (age). We have also gone through the three Beings of God known to us. Our aim in this chapter is to zoom in on the Being of God in charge today. To explain this, it is better we go through each dispensation from the origin. We will highlight the God of each age up until this present age.

In the beginning God...

Genesis 1:1 NLT says, *"in the beginning, God created the heavens and the earth."* When the scripture here says God, I believe the Bible was referring to God-the Father. In our previous discussion, we have established that the three Beings of God known to us are God-the Father, Jesus and the Holy Spirit. From the account of the Scriptures, the Father is often referred to as God. The Son is called Jesus, the Word (**John 1:1 & 14**), Lord (**Romans 10:9**), the Son of God (**Romans 1:4**) and the Son of Man (**Matthew 18:11**). The Holy Spirit is the Spirit of God (**Genesis 1:2**); some of the early Bible translations called Him the Holy Ghost.

From Genesis to Revelations, we see these name distinctions used in different situations. For example, God the Father and the Holy Spirit appeared physically while Jesus appeared as the word of the Father (**John 1**) in the beginning at creation. Jesus also appeared physically in **Daniel 3:25** before He was officially born on earth.

Genesis 1:1-3 NLT — *In the beginning, **God** created the heavens and the earth. The earth was formless and empty, and darkness covered the deep waters. And the **Spirit of God** was hovering over the surface of the waters. Then God said, "Let there be light," and there was light.*

Daniel 3:25 NKJV — *"Look!" he answered, "I see four men loose, walking in the midst of the fire; and they are not hurt, and the form of the fourth is like the **Son of God**."*

From the accounts of the Bible with regards to creation, we can say that God the Father is the God of creation. Depending on the biblical translation, God is often referred to when talking about the beginning and creation (**Hebrews 3:4, Jeremiah 32:17 KJV** and **Ephesians 2:10**).

Furthermore, God the Father is the primary existence of the Being of God as a whole. And because He is the creator, the God of the beginning and creation, He was, therefore, the God of that dispensation. The dispensation being referred to here started from creation to the early part of the new testament. Therefore, the people of that age consulted God-the Father through sacrifices, rituals and all other ways as laid out by the God of that age. In the early parts of the new testament, the Israelites were not finding it easy to let go of God-the Father and their approach to Him.

There were certain occurrences that happened in the old testament that we wouldn't have deemed appropriate today. Many individuals have put God and Christianity on trial because of this. We must not fail to understand that we live in a different dispensation that has a different approach to the same God.

To further our understanding of the age of God-the Father, let's look at this Biblical story together.

1 Chronicles 13:1-10 NLT — *David consulted with all his officials, including the generals and captains of his army. Then he addressed the entire assembly of Israel as follows: "If you approve and if it is the will of the Lord our God, let us send messages to all the Israelites throughout the land, including the priests and Levites in their towns and pasturelands. Let us invite them to come and join us. It is time to bring back the Ark of our God, for we neglected it during the reign of Saul." The whole assembly agreed to this, for the people could see it was the right thing to do. So, David summoned all Israel, from the Shihor Brook of Egypt in the south all the way to the town of Lebo-hamath in the north, to join in bringing the Ark of God from Kiriath-jearim. Then David and all Israel went to Baalah of Judah (also called Kiriath-jearim) to bring back the Ark of God, which bears the name of the Lord who is enthroned between the cherubim. They placed the Ark of God on a new cart and brought it from Abinadab's house. Uzzah and Ahio were guiding the cart. David and all Israel were celebrating before God with all their might, singing songs and playing all kinds of mu-*

sical instruments—lyres, harps, tambourines, cymbals, and trumpets. But when they arrived at the threshing floor of Nacon the oxen stumbled, and Uzzah reached out his hand to steady the Ark. Then the Lord's anger was aroused against Uzzah, and he struck him dead because he had laid his hand on the Ark. So Uzzah died there in the presence of God.

Obviously, this was a sad incident that happened during the dispensation of God-the Father. Unfortunately, this wasn't the only one (**Leviticus 10**). These incidents and many other anachronistic laws make us wonder if God-the Father was mean? The simple answer to that question is that God was not mean and here is why. In every dispensation, the God of that age can come in contact with the people of that age. In **Exodus 33:11**, God-the Father spoke to Moses face to face. We must remember that as per **Habakkuk 1:13**, God-the Father cannot look at sin or come into a sinful environment. Human nature had already been corrupted in the garden of Eden (**Genesis 3**); hence putting all in a default state of sin (**Romans 3:23**). Therefore, we understand that coming face to face or in contact with God the Father in our default nature is a very dangerous thing; unless we are cleansed. **Romans 6:23 NLT** says, *"for the wages of sin is death;"* the death being referred to in the age of God-the Father is both spiritual and physical death. In this age, the Priests appointed to preside over the sacrifices of others must cleanse themselves first, otherwise, physical death was inevitable. If a sinful person comes in contact with the Father's presence (i.e., the God of that age), they will die physically. This was the essence of the laws and purification listed in the age of God the Father. This is still true even today; however, our approach to God the Father is now different, as we find out soon.

Remember that God the Father is love (**1 John 4:8**) and He understands the circumstance. Due to this dilemma, the Father gave strict rules in that dispensation. He did this to mitigate the propensity of death and damage that could occur; when the [sinful] people of that age came in contact with Him. It is imperative to state that many things the people of the present age are getting away with, would have been impossible at that age.

Getting back to the passage we read earlier, we understand that the ark of God was significant in those days. This was because it represented, carried and contained the presence of God the Father. As such, where the ark was, God-the Father was present. As per **Deuteronomy 31:9**, the chosen Priests were entrusted with carrying the ark of the covenant of God. But notice that David and the Israelites placed the ark of God on a "new cart" instead of the shoulders of the Priests. To put this in perspective, all Israelites sinned by this act of disrespect and disobedience. Neither David nor the people followed the rules with regard to the ark. When a sinful Israelite named Uzzah came in close proximity to the presence of God the Father, he was struck dead. As per research, some Bible scholars actually believe there is a possibility that the man Uzzah was from the family of the Priests; hence his family could have been responsible for carrying the ark.

Now let's zoom out of the situation. Looking from the outside, it is easy to say well, God could have let that go. But as a matter of fact, the nature of God the Father is unforgiving when it comes to sin. We must understand this! It is not

God that kills but sin; unfortunately, the sinner is naturally consumed at the sight of God's presence. Just like, it is not gasoline that kills, but the presence of a heat source, which can cause significant damage. Remember, even Jesus-the Son, when He was on the cross carrying our sins, God had to look away (**Matthew 27:46**). Therefore, it is up to us to take precautionary measures as stated by God's law and stop allotting faults. When you come to the Father's presence, ensure you are without sin and you'll be fine, as we have seen severally in scriptures.

Now let's dig even deeper into the passage. With the help of the Holy Spirit, I noticed something fascinating in **1 Chronicles 13:10** of our Bible reading, *"Then the **Lord's** anger was aroused against Uzzah, and he struck him dead because he had laid his hand on the Ark. So Uzzah died there in the presence of **God**."* Did you see what I saw? Remember how I defined the three Beings of God known to us? Look at this. The Lord (not God) was angry, but Uzzah died there in the presence of God the Father. As per our discussion, Jesus is Lord. How was Jesus angry here? He wasn't even born yet? Here is the funny thing; I had always thought that the Bible used Lord and God interchangeably—after all both are one. But as per **Exodus 25:21**, the ark contained among many other things, the stone tablets inscribed with the terms of the covenant, which God gave the Israelites. Hence the ark contained the Word of God. We know from **John 1** that Jesus is the Word. Could this mean that the ark of the covenant also contained the presence of Jesus? In that case, it was Jesus that was ridiculed and humiliated by the disobedient acts of the Israelites. Therefore, it makes sense why the scripture will record that it was the

LORD (not God) that was angry. However, even though it was the Lord-Jesus that was angry, it was recorded that Uzzah died in the presence of God the Father, who was the God of that age. I believe the scripture added this last piece because though the Lord was angry, Uzzah died in the presence and with the consent of the God in charge. But who really struck Uzzah? Was it the Father or the Lord Jesus?

When the Bible stated that *"he struck him dead,"* a fair question will be, since *Uzzah died in the presence of **God***, who struck Uzzah to death? The "He" here could have been God or the Lord. The answer to that question is found in **2 Samuel 6:7 NLT** *(Then the **LORD**'s anger was aroused against Uzzah, and **God** struck him dead because of this. So Uzzah died right there beside the Ark of **God**).* It was clear from this second scripture that it was God-the Father that struck Uzzah dead. It makes sense because He was the God of that age. He had the right to act in that dispensation. To be clear, each Being of God is God. Therefore, Jesus could have acted, but He deferred to the God of that age as a matter of principle and respect. The Father took the lead in that dispensation. The action that was taken by God-the Father is consistent with His nature when He sees sin.

To conclude our analysis, we can see how things were done right, based on the lessons learned from the first incident—the death of Uzzah.

1 Chronicles 15:25-27 NLT — *Then David and the elders of Israel and the generals of the army went to the house of Obed-edom to bring the Ark of the Lord's Covenant up to Jerusalem with a great celebration.* **And because God was clearly helping the Levites as they carried the Ark of the Lord's Covenant,** *they sacrificed seven* *bulls and seven rams. David was dressed in a robe of fine linen, as were all the Levites who carried the Ark, and also the singers, and Kenaniah the choir leader. David was also wearing a priestly garment. So, all Israel brought up the Ark of the Lord's Covenant with shouts of joy, the blowing of rams' horns and trumpets, the crashing of cymbals, and loud playing on harps and lyres.*

And He will be called the Son of God

At the beginning of the New Testament, an angel was sent to declare the heart of God the Father for an imminent future. *The angel replied, "The Holy Spirit will come upon you, and the power of the Most High will overshadow you. So, the baby to be born will be holy, and he will be called the **Son of God***". (**Luke 1:35 NLT**)

As I mentioned earlier, God the Father recognizes the danger of our nature coming in contact with His. He gave us the law, but it wasn't enough. Instead, we kept drifting even farther away from Him. This hurt Him deeply. So, He decided that the best way was for Him to relate with us in a different way that was less dangerous for us. Hence the manifestation and revelation of His Being-Jesus. Therefore, during the dispensation of God the Father, He gave prophecies upon prophecies in preparation for the arrival of the next primary God. Starting from Moses to Isaiah, and many other prophets, the coming of the Messiah (Jesus) was well prophesied and publicized.

When the time came, Jesus was born of a virgin called Mary. He was born as a man, so we can relate with Him on a human level. He was also born of a virgin to preserve His divine nature. He was born as a baby and grew into a Man. However, He did not grow into being God, but He was born God. Jesus did not ascend His short reign on the earth immediately. This happened when He grew into a man; He was about 30 years old. This simply means that when Jesus was born and before His ministry started, He was also under the dispensation of God the Father. That is, He was bound by the rules and regulations. We were made to understand that Jesus was sinless throughout His life (**1 Peter 2:22 and 2 Corinthians 5:21**). This can only mean that He followed and obeyed the rules of the dispensation He was born into. This is because, in **Matthew 5:17 NLT**, Jesus said, *"Don't misunderstand why I have come. I did not come to abolish the law of Moses or the writings of the prophets. No, I came to accomplish their purpose."* In **Romans 13:8-10**, we see how the law and the writings of the prophets accomplish their purpose.

Romans 13:8-10 NLT — *Owe nothing to anyone—except for your obligation to love one another. If you love your neighbor, you will fulfill the requirements of God's law. For the commandments say, "You must not commit adultery. You must not murder. You must not steal. You must not covet." These—and other such commandments—are summed up in this one commandment: "Love your neighbor as yourself." Love does no wrong to others, so love fulfills the requirements of God's law.*

And as established earlier, it was during the dispensation of Jesus that He reinforced the law of love (**Matthew 22:37-39**). Jesus is, therefore, the fulfillment of God the Father. As such, He had to wait until He was incumbent (i.e., for the Father to usher in His dispensation).

The short dispensation of Jesus on earth officially started

when these words, *"This is my dearly loved Son, who brings me great joy."* were uttered by the Father in **Matthew 3:17**. These words marked the beginning of Jesus' short earthly dispensation. It is imperative to know that Jesus' dispensation was created for one purpose—to create a safe doorway to God-the Father that is without fear and endangerment. Just like every good organization, there is always a transitory period between an outgoing and incoming postholder, during which a final handover occurs. This was exactly what happened between the dispensations of God-the Father and Jesus. From the birth of Jesus to His baptism, I dubbed it the transitory period. The baptism, however, marks the handover. God the Father spoke from heaven to let everyone know that Jesus (the Son) was the primary God on earth henceforth; consequently, Jesus' dispensation began.

From that moment up until Pentecost in **Acts 2**, Jesus was the primary Being of God on earth. Anything God communicated went through Jesus, who personified God (**Colossians 2:9**). God the Father took the back seat, while Jesus took the front seat. Even though Jesus was in the front seat, God-the Father still remained the commander of all. Jesus said *"I tell you the truth, the Son can do nothing by himself. He does only what he sees the Father doing. Whatever the Father does, the Son also does"* (**John 5:19 NLT**). For that reason, the Father remained the God of all in every dispensation; however, He took the backseat for the sake of humanity. Jesus was basically tailored for our needs; we are all feeble creatures in need of a savior like us. Jesus is God's custom channel for us to come back to Him. The one we can touch, feel and relate to. God the Father in the form of His Son (Jesus), left His glory to satisfy this need of ours.

Philippians 2:7-8 NLT — *Instead, he gave up his divine privileges; he took the humble position of a slave and was born as a human being. When he appeared in human form, he humbled himself in obedience to God and died a criminal's death on a cross.*

In the Bible, we must have noticed some people called the Scribes, Pharisees and Sadducees in the time of Jesus. These people have been painted with a hypocritical brush over the years; their acts during the dispensation of Jesus fueled this perspective. However, believe it or not, some of these people were genuine servants of God; they simply lacked understanding. Some were only trying to uphold the law that God-the Father gave through Moses. I am inclined to believe that, perhaps, some of them missed the public handover ceremony of God-the Father to Jesus. Remember, Jesus came to fulfill the goal of God-the Father's dispensation. This was what these people failed to realize. They were still hung up on the past dispensation and they wanted to operate the same way in the new dispensation. They attacked Jesus at every opportunity, believing they were doing the work of God. How sad! The truth is, there are many Pharisees in the world today (i.e., within the context of mindset).

But the Advocate, the Holy Spirit…

When it was about time for Jesus to die, He started preparing His disciples for the next course of action. He enthused over the imminent coming of the Holy Spirit and told

His disciples to expect Him. In many instances, Jesus was crystal clear about the coming of the Holy Spirit.

John 16:7 NLT — *But in fact, it is best for you that I go away, because if I don't, the Advocate won't come. If I do go away, then I will send him to you.*

At this moment in scripture, Jesus' words (especially in **John 16**) seemed as though He was in the transitory period and getting ready for a handover. According to **Luke 24:46 NLT**, *"And he said, 'Yes, it was written long ago that the Messiah would suffer and die and rise from the dead on the third day.'"* It is therefore part of Jesus' calling to die. His death is what opened the door of salvation to us. It was after He died that He was able to go down to hell—to take back everything that was stolen from us and secure our victory. He came back triumphant and victorious. Hallelujah!

Matthew 28:18 NLT — *Jesus came and told his disciples, "I have been given all authority in heaven and on earth."*

1 Corinthians 15:55-57 NLT — *O death, where is your victory? O death, where is your sting?" For sin is the sting that results in death, and the law gives sin its power. But thank God! He gives us victory over sin and death through our Lord Jesus Christ.*

Let's have a recap. The Father handed over to Jesus. He did this so that we can come to Him through Jesus without danger. As part of this, Jesus had to die to clear the way and become an atonement for our sin (**2 Corinthians 5:21 NLT**). After death, He is to be seated in heaven at the right hand of the Father pleading our case (**Romans 8:34**). But as I mentioned earlier, there is a need for a Being of God in every dispensation, because we are made alive by the breath of God

(**Genesis 2:7**). His breath comes from His presence; hence we need His presence at all times, here on earth.

The short dispensation of Jesus ended at Pentecost in **Acts 2**. Even though Jesus finished His work and left the earth, this did not stop the devil from actively working to steal, kill and destroy (**John 10:10**). We could not be left alone on earth with the devil traversing. Therefore, Jesus started proclaiming the coming of the next Being of God before His age was over. Just as there were so many prophecies about the Messiah (Jesus) in the dispensation of the Father, Jesus announced and prophesied about the Holy Spirit. He did this, particularly when it was close to the time of His departure.

An incident happened in scripture that I will like us to look into. In **Acts 1:8 NLT**, Jesus told the disciples, *"But you will receive power when the Holy Spirit comes upon you. And you will be my witnesses, telling people about me everywhere-in Jerusalem, throughout Judea, in Samaria, and to the ends of the earth."* I see this last act of Jesus (after His resurrection) as His official handover to the Holy Spirit. Jesus announced the Holy Spirit to His disciples, just like God-the Father announced Him (during His baptism).

After the death of Jesus, the disciples were confused. Some of them had no idea what to do. They retrogressed to fishing, which connoted going back to their old life (**John 21:3**). Yes, they heard Jesus talk about the coming of the Holy Spirit, but they had no idea how and where to receive Him. They were so accustomed to Jesus' leadership that the thought of having another master scared them. What they failed to understand was *"the glory of the latter is greater than the former"* (**Haggai 2:9**). Moreover, they had no idea that the Father, Jesus and the

Holy Spirit were one and the same. Consequently, Jesus had to come back, to enable their understanding of the importance of the forthcoming dispensation. Jesus' word in **Acts 1:8** was meant for us all. I have demystified it as, *"To get anything done in this new age, you need power; you must also understand that there is a new sheriff in town, He is the Holy Spirit. You must relate more with Him, otherwise, you will be kicking against God's approach for this new dispensation."*

Pharisees today?

Recollecting scriptural accounts and what I earlier alluded to, many of us don't understand the Pharisees and the other cohorts during the time of Jesus. Some of us see them as hypocrites. This is a fair assessment from our point of view. Their acts, behaviors and mannerisms portrayed them as such. However, we must understand that some of these people were actually servants of God. Yes, there were instances that they were used by the devil. This was only possible because they were kicking against God's agenda for that time.

The Pharisees and co were experts in the laws of Moses and its ways. They have devoted their time, effort and energy to please God in this way. However, the issue was that God had left that bus and was currently on the bus of Jesus (at that time). As I had mentioned, they probably missed the handover ceremony at Jesus' baptism. The sin that made them tools in the devil's hand was this: their conformance to the ways established for the dispensation of the Father during the dispensation of the Son. Hence, they were swimming against the tides. This made them vulnerable because they were not in line with God and therefore not under His covering. It was so bad that when it was time for the messiah to die, the devil actually used them as an instrument to kill Jesus (**John 19:15**). The fact was that Jesus was going to die anyway, but the Pharisees didn't have to be accomplices. Of course, the devil was completely ignorant that killing Jesus was just an element of God's grand agenda (**1 Corinthians 2:8**).

Do you know that we still have people like the Pharisees today? You say how? Here is the deal. Jesus handed over to the Holy Spirit at the end of His short dispensation. In the same manner, the Father handed it over to Him. However, there are some people today who have failed to believe in the Holy Spirit. They have been surreptitiously blindfolded by the devil into believing the Holy Spirit is of the devil. A Spirit? So, He must be spooky, they say. Wake up! That is a lie from the pit of hell. *God is Spirit, so those who worship him must worship in spirit and in truth* (**John 4:24 NLT**). How do you intend to worship God in Spirit without His Holy Spirit? Remember, it was Jesus that came back to tell the disciple about the Holy Spirit one last time in **Acts 1:8**. There is no confusion here; any so-called way to God that does not involve the Holy Spirit is ***false***. Because after salvation, which is coming to God through the door**way** of Jesus (**John 10:9**), the Holy Spirit is the stair**way** to the Father. One step after another, He is making us into a perfect bride of God (**Ephesian 5:27**). Our relationship with the Father through Jesus is only sustained by the Holy Spirit. Therefore, the scriptures say in this current dispensation, "only those that *are led by the **Spirit of God** are children of God*" (**Romans 8:14 NLT**). Hence after salvation, we are expected to move onto the stairway and take the first step of our journey to perfection. Anyone still at the door, that is, salvation through Jesus without consciously building a relationship with the Holy Spirit is a Pharisee of today. And as such, susceptible to the devil's use. Move past salvation, the doorway and plug into the Holy Spirit; this is the way of God for this dispensation.

4

The God of this Age

Now that we have identified that the God of this age is the Holy Spirit, it is therefore important to drill down into understanding Him. Let's dive in.

Who is the Holy Spirit?

The Holy Spirit is simply the Spirit of God the Father. He is called Holy because God the Father to whom He belongs is Holy (**1 Peter 1:16** & **Leviticus 19:2**). This, therefore, makes Him Holy as well. As the Spirit of God the Father, He has every capability of God. So, it is safe to say everything that what God is capable of, the Holy Spirit is as well.

Over the course of many dispensations, the Holy Spirit has been there at every move of God-the Father; He was there at creation (**Genesis 1:2**); He was there throughout the dispensation of God the Father (**Judges 3:10, Isaiah 61:1, 1 Samuel 16:13 and Ezekiel 11:5**); He was there during the time of Jesus (**Luke 3:22**). He had played a supporting role all through these dispensations. However, in this day and age, the Holy Spirit is the primary God.

From this point on, I will refer to God the Father as God. To help us understand the Holy Spirit, we will examine the closest being to the nature of God on earth today. Our nature is the closest to God's. As mentioned in Chapter 2, we are created in the image of God. As such, our best chance of understanding the Holy Spirit will be to look at our nature. Apostle Paul in **1 Corinthians 2:11 NLT** shared a part of our nature that corresponds with God's. He said, *"no one can know a person's thoughts except that person's own spirit, and no one can know God's thoughts except God's own Spirit."* From this verse, we see the intricacy of a person's spirit. The spirit is a very sacred and intimate part of a person. Neither God nor us can hide from our spirit. Based on this insight, we can say that the Holy Spirit is the custodian of God's thoughts. Hence the Holy Spirit is very significant if we are to obey God.

Names are given as an identifier and qualifiers. If we are to know the God of this age (the Holy Spirit), it is only wise that we explore some of His names in the scriptures. In doing so, we may see some significance attached to His name.

The Holy Spirit—His Names

The Spirit of God

Genesis 1:2 NLT — *The earth was formless and empty, and darkness covered the deep waters. And **the Spirit of God** was hovering over the surface of the waters.*

The Bible here described Him as the Spirit of God. This

makes Him God. He is a Person of God Being. Over the years, we have seen people describe the Holy Spirit as "it;" this is not just inaccurate, but flat-out disrespectful. However, as humans, we are more prone to the physical. When occurrences are beyond our ability to grasp, we are inclined towards unconcern and conjecture. The same is applicable here, the early scholars could not attribute the work, move and nature of the Spirit of God to any gender, so they qualified Him as it. They had no clue who or what was moving (**John 3:8**). It wasn't the God they were used to. But as we gained more revelation and understanding, we now know that the Spirit of God is God, and must be qualified as such. Therefore, as the Spirit of a man is the man in all sense, the Spirit of God is God.

The Seven Spirits of God

In getting to know the God of this age (the Holy Spirit), there is a significant aspect that must be considered. The Bible alluded to something that almost seems untenable in the book of Revelations about the Spirit of God.

Revelations 1:4 NKJV — *John, to the seven churches which are in Asia: Grace to you and peace from Him who is and who was and who is to come, and from **the seven Spirits** who are before His throne.*

Revelations 4:5 NKJV — *And out of the throne come flashes of lightning, and voices, and thundering. And there were seven lamps of fire burning before the throne, which are **the seven Spirits of God**.*

We see the Bible refer to the Seven Spirits of God. So, does this mean God has seven Spirits? And going by the logic of 2

Corinthians 13:1 and **Deuteronomy 19:15**, this has been established twice. So, we can say this is true. If this is true, which one of these seven Spirits is the God of this age? In answering this question, I want to implore you to pay closer attention. Let's look at another scripture where it seems as though the Bible committed an English language blunder. In

Galatians 5:22-23 NLT — *But the Holy Spirit produces this kind of fruit in our lives: love, joy, peace, patience, kindness, goodness, faithfulness, gentleness, and self-control. There is no law against these things!*

The Bible referred to love, joy, peace, patience, kindness, goodness, faithfulness, gentleness, and self-control as one fruit. Yes, not fruits but fruit. Look at it again. Every translation is like that. Did you notice that despite all these goodies, the Bible referred to all of them as fruit, not fruits? This is because all of these good things come from one Spirit, the Holy Spirit. Many Christians don't realize this, but it is only one fruit that is produced from one Spirit. There are nine goodies from this one fruit, and all these nine goodies are in the Holy Spirit. Because of this, the Holy Spirit can be referred to as the Spirit of any of these goodies (such as the Spirit of love, the Spirit of goodness, et al.). You will still be referring to just one Spirit with all kinds of great names, based on what you know of Him at a particular time. Once you have the Holy Spirit you have it all. However, you can pick and choose what you want the Holy Spirit to help activate and cultivate, which is what you'll then operate in.

Going back to the seven Spirits of God, the New Living Translation of the Bible referred to what the New King James

Version called seven Spirits as the sevenfold Spirit consistently in these two scriptures.

Revelations 1:4 NLT — *This letter is from John to the seven churches in the province of Asia. Grace and peace to you from the one who is, who always was, and who is still to come; from **the sevenfold Spirit** before his throne.*

Revelations 4:5 NLT — *From the throne came flashes of lightning and the rumble of thunder. And in front of the throne were seven torches with burning flames. This is **the sevenfold Spirit of God**.*

This clarifies things better and corroborates my earlier account. Furthermore, it is a consensus among Bible scholars that this was an indication of the Spirit of God being a perfect Spirit. This is so because the number seven is a significant Biblical number that often denotes perfection and completion.

Genesis 2:1-3 NLT — *So the creation of the heavens and the earth and everything in them was completed. On the seventh day God had finished his work of creation, so he rested from all his work. And God blessed the seventh day and declared it holy, because it was the day when he rested from all his work of creation.*

We may have noticed that each time the seven Spirits were mentioned, there is a preceding seven. In **Revelation 1:4**, it was to the seven churches; in **Revelation 4:5**, it was the seven torches. This simply means each of the Spirits corresponds to each church and torch. This is crucial because, when Isaiah was prophesying about Jesus, he listed the seven Spirits that will be upon Jesus.

Isaiah 11:2 NLT — *And the **Spirit of the LORD** will rest on* him— the **Spirit of wisdom** and **understanding**, the **Spirit of counsel** and **might**, the **Spirit of knowledge** and the **fear of the LORD**.

These seven Spirits are the seven spirits in the book of Revelations, and to this, a majority of Bible scholars concur. Now let's know more about the God of this age from the lenses of these seven Spirits.

The Spirit of the LORD

Jesus Christ is Lord (**Philippians 2:11** and **1 Corinthians 8:6**). Therefore, the Spirit of God is the Spirit of Christ.

Romans 8:9 NLT — *But you are not controlled by your sinful nature. You are controlled by the Spirit if you have the Spirit of God living in you. (And remember that those who do not have **the Spirit of Christ** living in them do not belong to him at all.)*

As explained in Chapter 2, Jesus Christ is the Son of God. This Being of God was revealed for our sake. God came as the Son to save us. Jesus is God's custom remedy to humanity's problem of sin caused by the first people (**Genesis 3**). Jesus Christ is God and part of God's Being. The Spirit of God is therefore the Spirit of Jesus Christ.

Jesus being Lord makes the Spirit He carries the Spirit of the Lord. We must also remember that God the Father, Jesus and the Holy Spirit are one. So, when we say the Spirit of God, the Spirit of Jesus Christ or the Spirit of the Lord, we are referring to one and the same Spirit.

The question that arises here then becomes, if the Spirit is that of Christ, why did Isaiah prophesy that the Spirit will rest on Him? This prophecy was demonstrated when the Holy Spirit descended like a dove on Jesus (**Luke 3:22**). When a spirit descends on a person, either good or evil, the spirit becomes an attribute of that person. For example, God breathed into Adam in **Genesis 2:7** and he became a living being. Hence the breath of God in us becomes the spirit in us that makes us alive. This wasn't ours originally but God's. However, the moment it came into us, it became our attribute. Even though it is our attribute, it still longs for its source—God, and this is why we need God.

The Bible said something interesting in **1 Corinthians 14:32 NKJV**, *"And the spirits of the prophets are subject to the prophets."* In this passage, Apostle Paul was writing to the Church of Corinth; the Spirit of Prophecy being referred to in this passage is from God. Did you notice that it was attributed to the carrier, in this case, the Prophets? There was another similar event in the old testament.

2 Kings 2:15 NLT — *When the group of prophets from Jericho saw from a distance what happened, they exclaimed, "Elijah's spirit rests upon Elisha!" And they went to meet him and bowed to the ground before him.*

This was when Elisha received a double portion of Elijah's spirit. The Spirit that Elisha received was associated with the previous carrier of the Spirit, Elijah. Therefore, the moment the Holy Spirit came upon Jesus, the Spirit became the Spirit of the Lord Jesus.

The Spirit of Wisdom

Proverbs 4:7 NKJV — *Wisdom is the principal thing; Therefore, get wisdom. And in all your getting, get understanding.*

The importance of wisdom is highlighted in the scripture

above. It is the most important virtue that can create ease in one's life. One anointed vessel of the Lord defines wisdom as the *correct* application of knowledge. I simply define wisdom as the ability to know the right thing and do it at the right time.

From Chapter 1, we know that the recipe for wisdom is understanding and that of understanding is knowledge. The Holy Spirit is the Spirit of Wisdom because He is God. He has the knowledge and understanding of all things; this makes Him indispensable. Since He made it all, He understands it all and knows it all. Knowing the right thing to do and the right time to do it can only come from Him. This makes Him the source and giver of wisdom. When instructions are given by the Holy Spirit, they are given out of the depth of God's knowledge to help us in situations. When revelations are given by the Holy Spirit, they are given out of the vault of His understanding to give us the wisdom required for situations.

We notice this same thing in people with the Spirit of Wisdom. This was evident in Jesus; in **Matthew 19**, He was tested, but He successfully dealt with that situation without falling into any trap. Other than Jesus, Solomon (in the old testament) was the wisest man that ever lived; in **1 Kings 3:16-28**, the Spirit of Wisdom in him was put to test and he excelled. In this world we live in, the devil has successfully convinced some people that being ruthless is the only way to get ahead in life. Because of this deception, the Spirit of Wisdom is even more important in this day and age. The Holy Spirit is the God of this age and also the Spirit of Wisdom. Knowing and having a relationship with Him is the only straightforward way to the top.

The Spirit of Understanding

Since understanding is a recipe for wisdom, it only makes sense that the Spirit of Wisdom is also the Spirit of Understanding. If wisdom is the correct application of knowledge, then we must understand what we are applying. As explained in Chapter 1, nothing becomes true to us until we understand it. The Holy Spirit gives us the right analogies and revelations; He also reveals things to us to enhance our understanding. Jesus said that the Holy Spirit will teach us everything.

John 14:26 NLT — *But, when the Father sends the Advocate as my representative—that is, the Holy Spirit—he will teach you everything and will remind you of everything I have told you.*

The purpose of teaching is for us to assimilate information and gain understanding. The role of the Holy Spirit makes Him the Spirit that brings and gives understanding.

The Spirit of Counsel

Counsel simply means to give advice; this is another qualification of the Holy Spirit. Because He knows everything and is the only dwelling presence of God on the earth today, the Holy Spirit is well-positioned to give us advice in every situation. He can effectively do this because He knows the heart of God.

1 Corinthians 2:11 NLT — *No one can know a person's*

thoughts except that person's own spirit, and no one can know God's thoughts except God's own Spirit.

One of the challenges we face as human is that in some situations, we have little or no insight into the will of God. The devil knows this, so he comes to give us false information—deception. There are some things that are written explicitly in the Bible, but there are others that require inside information from the heart of God. For example, it is very clear from Scripture that we cannot steal and we must love our neighbor. But what happens when I am trying to move to a new city? Figuring out if it is the will of God or not will require an answer from God. In some cases, the answer might be in the Bible; however, such answers require a different kind of revelation that only the Holy Spirit can give. These are the awesome accesses we have to God through the counsel of the Holy Spirit.

The Spirit of Might

Might, which means power is the ability to do something. This means for things to get done, power is needed. There are all kinds of power, but we will focus on two major kinds of power—physical and spiritual. The physical gives our body the ability to get things done—in a very basic sense, a healthy person can get things done. On the other hand, spiritual power gives us the ability to get things done in the spiritual realm. Since we are naturally physical beings, we often pay more attention to physical power and neglect the Spiritual. Many eat healthy and go to the gym to take care of their physical being while ignoring the spiritual. We can acquire physical power without help; however, we definitely need help for the spiritual side of things. Some might even ask, why do I need spiritual strength? We will explore this.

Some might think because the Spirit of God is a spirit being, everything about Him (including the power He gives) is solely spiritual. Not quite true, He does supply spiritual strength, but He also gives physical strength.

Judges 14:6 NLT — *At that moment the Spirit of the LORD came powerfully upon him [Samson], and he ripped the lion's jaws apart with his bare hands. He did it as easily as if it were a young goat. But he didn't tell his father or mother about it.*

We can see an unusual physical power fell upon Samson, without his going to the gym and he did the impossible. Some may argue that Samson was a special man created for this purpose. This is true, but it is also applicable to everyone in this dispensation. There is only one thing that distinguished Samson in His time. He was privileged to operate in these aspects of the Holy Spirit in the dispensation of the Father. Since we are in the dispensation of the Holy Spirit, we have access to even more physical and spiritual might. To further explain the power the Holy Spirit gives, let's consider this scripture.

Acts 1:8 NLT — *But you will receive power when the Holy Spirit comes upon you. And you will be my witnesses, telling people about me everywhere-in Jerusalem, throughout Judea, in Samaria, and to the ends of the earth.*

Jesus' words in **Acts 1:8** clearly portray that the Holy Spirit is associated with power. In this verse of scripture, we can see why power is needed to fulfil the instructions of Jesus. Jesus made it very clear that we cannot be His witnesses until we receive power from the Holy Spirit. We might be wondering, "telling various people about Jesus is quite simple, why does Jesus think we need the power of the Holy Spirit here?"

First off, physical power (which also includes mental, emotional and so on) is needed to move around and spread the good news about Jesus. We cannot fulfil this scripture if we are sick or a weakling. Hence the salvation work of Jesus gives us access to the divine health and vitality that comes from the physical power of the Holy Spirit. (**Isaiah 53:5**).

It is actually possible to be sickness-free. Even though we have access to divine health and vitality through the Holy Spirit, we also have a role to play. We are to take on requisite actions for vigor, such as living a healthy lifestyle and ingesting a balanced diet. The Holy Spirit will not help us if we are unwilling. Living a healthy lifestyle is a sign of our willingness and commitment. It is within our capability; therefore, God will not do this for us. However, this alone does not guarantee good health and vitality. It is the power of the Holy Spirit coupled with our willingness that does.

Secondly, telling people about Jesus is one of the hardest things to do. The devil has strategically made sure that we can freely talk about God but not Jesus. You may have noticed in several contexts that once the name Jesus comes up, many people begin to shrink back. In some workplaces, discussions about Jesus are prohibited. God is generic so it's fine, but Jesus is too specific. The Bible tells us in **Philippians 2:10** that at the mention of the name of Jesus every knee must bow. Even demons are uncomfortable when we set out to talk about Jesus. Therefore, spiritual power is needed, because the enemies we are fighting against are not flesh and blood.

Ephesians 6:12 NLT — *For we are not fighting against flesh-*

and-blood enemies, but against evil rulers and authorities of the unseen world, against mighty powers in this dark world, and against evil spirits in the heavenly places.

The Spirit of Knowledge

The dictionary defines knowledge as facts, information, and skills acquired by a person through experience or education. If we agree with this definition, it simply means that the Spirit of knowledge is the Spirit of facts, information and skills. Though this is true, I want to be very clear that the Holy Spirit is not an excuse to be lazy. His intention is to give us the grace to go beyond our capacity. The Bible reveals in **2 Corinthians 12:9** that grace is always available when it is needed. Until things get beyond our capacity, the Holy Spirit might not step in.

2 Corinthians 12:9 NLT — *Each time he said, "My grace is all you need. My power works best in weakness." So now I am glad to boast about my weaknesses, so that the power of Christ can work through me.*

The Spirit of God provides us with facts, information and skills when needed because *it was to us that God revealed these things by his Spirit. For his Spirit* **searches out everything and shows us God's deep secrets** (**1 Corinthians 2:10 NLT**). Remember, the Holy Spirit is God and as such, He knows it all. Our first line of action to acquire success is to gather facts, information and skills. There is no better person to give us these things other than the one who knows it all and searches the deep secrets of God.

The latter part of our definition of knowledge specified

that its acquisition was "through experience and education." Experiences are occurrences that we go through. This is so important because the Spirit of God is God and has been in existence from the beginning. He has all the experiences we will ever need. As such He is the wealth of knowledge. Also, oftentimes, He will allow certain things to occur, so we can acquire a requisite knowledge. Once we have gathered the pertinent information, as our teacher, He could further educate on the same topic or a similar one. For example, there was a trend I noticed in my own walk with God. Oftentimes, certain revelation does not come to me until I have received certain words from my spiritual father. God drops a piece of information into my spiritual father, and since it is in my capacity to get it from him, God will not share it with me. However, He will orchestrate an event that will lead me towards getting the information. The moment I gain the bedrock of the knowledge, He swoops in to build on that. Another way we can acquire knowledge is through the preaching and teachings at church. As the word of God goes forth, many people are gaining deeper insights and revelations beyond what is being preached or taught.

I cannot stress this fact enough. The Holy Spirit will not do for you what you can do for yourself. However, He will orchestrate events and bring opportunities for you to do what you are capable of doing. His grace is often for beyond-your-capacity realms. He is our helper, not our slave, He is there to help us in times of need (for those who want His help), and He is willing to take us beyond our capacity.

The Fear of God

The Bible says in **2 Timothy 1:7 NLT**, *"For God has not given us a spirit of fear and timidity, but of power, love, and self-discipline."* Fear is a spirit and it is not of God. However, there is an exception; the fear that the Holy Spirit gives. The word "fear" is used because the English language is limited. There are certain things we experience in God that words cannot effectively express. Hence, we look for the closest word in our vocabulary to express it; the "fear of God" is one of such. The fear of God simply means to be in awe (absolute respect) of God due to His capabilities. This is the same feeling we experience when we realize our parents are more powerful and influential than we initially thought, especially from someone close to us. Most likely, we will say, "Oh! My parents are very powerful?" This is because we just realized in our minds what that truly means. And consequently, our respect for them naturally increases. This respect is what is referred to as awe and oftentimes the feeling that accompanies it cannot be effectively expressed by any word.

The Spirit of God is the Fear of God because He gives us insight into God. We must understand that *"the secret things belong to the LORD our God, but those things which are revealed belong to us and to our children forever, that we may do all the words of this law"* (**Deuteronomy 29:29 NKJV**). These secrets are then released by the Holy Spirit (**1 Corinthians 2:10**) to those that He deems worthy. **Psalm 25:14 NKJV** says, *"the secret of the LORD is with those who fear Him, And He will show them His covenant."* Oh! Does God have secrets? Of course, He does, and who else will know those secrets if not His Spirit?

The more of those secrets that are revealed to us, the more of God we know, and the more respect we have for God. Knowing God more shows us more of His awesomeness. We are drawn into a state of awe that renders us speechless. For example, when we realize that the same God who is love (**1 John 4:8**) is also a consuming fire (**Hebrews 12:29**), it will give us a different kind of understanding and awe for Him.

The good thing about this is that the more of God's awesomeness we see, the more respect we have for God and the more aversion we have for sin. Under normal circumstances, when a reasonable person realizes that one of their parents is the President of the United States, their first instinct will be good conduct and a commitment to do what is right. They quickly realize that all eyes are on them, because of their relationship with the President. This is the same with our relationship with God through the Holy Spirit. If you believe that what was revealed to you by the Holy Spirit about God is compelling you to do bad, I am candidly telling you that is not God, neither was it revealed to you by His Spirit. Rebuke that demon and move on.

The Spirit of Truth

John 16:13 NLT — *When **the Spirit of truth** comes, he will guide you into all truth. He will not speak on his own but will tell you what he has heard. He will tell you about the future.*

As explained in Chapter 1, when a fact or belief (i.e., knowledge) has been tested, understanding comes. Once this happens, it can then be applied to situations as needed, which is deemed wisdom. Subsequently, it is established as the truth.

Truth goes through extensive testing and analysis; therefore, nothing becomes true to us unless we understand it. It is the truth that we acquire that sets us in motion.

Jesus said in **John 8:32 NLT,** *"And you will know the truth, and the truth will set you free."* In **Psalm 119:105 NLT**, the Bible made us understand that the word of God is both a lamp and light, that is, it is a source of illumination. We all know that light is the prerequisite for freedom; there is no freedom in darkness. If the word is light, and the truth sets us free, then at some point the word must become the truth to gain freedom. However, words are just facts until the Spirit of God guides us into the truth of the Word (i.e., grants us understanding). Anybody can read the word of God, but not everybody is guided into the truth. The Spirit brings understanding that helps us transform the word into the truth we need for our freedom. Therefore, the Spirit of God is associated with freedom and liberty— *For the Lord is the Spirit, and wherever the Spirit of the Lord is, there is freedom* (**2 Corinthians 3:17 NLT**).

The Advocate

John 15:26 NLT — *But I will send you the Advocate—the Spirit of truth. He will come to you from the Father and will testify all about me.*

From the scripture above, we see that the Holy Spirit was referred to as the Spirit of truth and the Advocate. Let us zoom in on Advocate. This is so interesting because the Bible made us understand that Jesus is currently seated at the right hand of the Father pleading our case—Advocating (**1 John**

2:1). This means Jesus is pleading our case to the Father in heaven, while the Holy Spirit is pleading our case to the Father on earth. Hence, we are covered and there is nothing to worry about. There is no more condemnation for us, either in heaven or on earth.

Romans 8:1 NLT — *So, now there is no condemnation for those who belong to Christ Jesus.*

Jesus pleads our case daily in front of the Father in heaven. But how does the Holy Spirit advocate for us here on earth? The scripture below opens up our eyes to one of the ways the Spirit advocates our case here on earth.

Luke 12:11-12 NLT — *"And when you are brought to trial in the synagogues and before rulers and authorities, don't worry about how to defend yourself or what to say, for the Holy Spirit will teach you at that time what needs to be said."*

As we may know, an advocate or a lawyer is often required to represent a defendant in a court of law. When the case of a defendant is being pled, every utterance matters. By saying either the right things or wrong things, an advocate orchestrates the acquittal or conviction of a defendant, respectively. Hence a guilty person can be acquitted of their charges if their advocate knows the right things to say.

Here is an insight. When we sin, we become an enemy of God. However, that automatically changes the moment we repent. This instantaneous change after repentance is the result of the salvation work of Jesus Christ and His advocacy at the right hand of the Father. However, the ongoing battle on earth has not ceased. Attacks and trials by the accuser of the brethren are inevitable (**Revelation 12:10**). These attacks are often perpetrated against our minds—both inside and outside. For example, an individual might struggle with believing they have been forgiven by God after repentance. This is within the courtroom of their mind. If the individual does not do the right things, they get onto a slippery slope to their own undoing and consequently grant access to the devil. Many, who have neglected or ignored the advocacy of the Holy Spirit, have fallen into great predicaments or backslid. The Holy Spirit in His all-knowing wisdom knows what to say, the treasures of God, and the principle of God from the Bible to engage in any circumstance. This is the freedom we enjoy through the advocacy of the Holy Spirit.

Prayer is an avenue to plead our case before God here on earth. Therefore, it is reasonable that our advocate here on earth (the Holy Spirit) will help us in our prayers. Because the Holy Spirit is connected to our own spirit (**Romans 8:16**), He knows our thoughts and desires (**1 Corinthians 2:11**). Hence, He (the Holy Spirit) can effectively advocate for us, by praying with us and for us (**Romans 8:26**).

Romans 8:16 NLT — *For his Spirit joins with our spirit to affirm that we are God's children.*

1 Corinthians 2:11 NLT — *No one can know a person's thoughts except that person's own spirit, and no one can know God's thoughts except God's own Spirit.*

Romans 8:26 NLT — *And the Holy Spirit helps us in our weakness. For example, we don't know what God wants us to pray for. But the Holy Spirit prays for us with groanings that cannot be expressed in words.*

5

Understanding the God of this Age

We will start this chapter by discussing the importance of the God of this age. There are countless benefits to having the Spirit of God. Therefore, it is simply impossible to write it all in one book. Even the Bible does not contain the entire capabilities of the Holy Spirit. As the God of this age, His capacity is unlimited, so also is His benefits. Starting from His ever-present help to His daily release of revelations, He is humorous and more than enough. But I will highlight a few benefits of the Holy Spirit within this book.

He Let Us Know the Will of God

As Children of God, our goal is to please God. In doing this, there are certain things that we must do to effectively please God; one of those is knowing the will of God. We can only strive to do God's will if we know what they are. Some are explicitly stated in the Word of God (The Bible), while others are not as clear. In cases of unclarity, we must rely on someone who can tell us the heart of God. According to **1 Corinthians 2:11 NLT,** *"No one can know a person's thoughts except that person's own spirit, and no one can know God's thoughts except God's own Spirit."* It is only a person's spirit that is exposed to a person's thoughts. From the name, we can see that the Holy Spirit is the Spirit of God; as such, He knows God's thoughts and God's will.

The Bible tells us in **Romans 8:16 NLT**, *"for his Spirit joins with our spirit to affirm that we are God's children."* Hence the moment we become saved, we receive a dose of the Holy Spirit, and He is connected to our spirit. So, His conviction ministry is in operation in us.

Acts 2:38 NLT — *Peter replied, "Each of you must repent of your sins and turn to God, and be baptized in the name of Jesus Christ for the forgiveness of your sins. Then you will receive the gift of the Holy Spirit.*

As such, the Holy Spirit is exposed to our every thought and He also knows the thoughts of God. The Holy Spirit exposes us to the thoughts of God as needed. In this way, we are always receiving God's Word in season. This is also one of the many reasons why often time we experience God's thoughts flow into our thoughts easily, like a spontaneous thought out of the blue. This is one of God's effective ways of talking to us.

1 John 5:14 NLT says, *"and we are confident that he hears us whenever we ask for anything that pleases God."* This scripture shows that our prayer is sure to be answered, only when we ask for things that please God. How do we know what pleases

God? Well, the Holy Spirit helps with that as explained earlier.

The Bible says in **James 4:3 NLT**, *"even when you ask, you don't get it because your motives are all wrong—you want only what will give you pleasure.* Our motives can only be right when we pray with the Holy Spirit. This is because, when necessary, the Holy Spirit sifts our motives by testing the content of our hearts in accordance with the will of God (**Deuteronomy 8:2** and **1 Corinthians 2:10**). He then presents us with the evidence of the problem (if any) and the solution. In doing so, when we approach God in prayer, we do so with the right heart posture and right motive. In addition to motives, the Holy Spirit also helps us in praying the right prayer in accordance with the will of God. (**Romans 8:26**). Because of this, we are always sure to have our prayers answered.

He Will Convict the World of Sin

When Jesus was promising the Holy Spirit, He said in **John 16:8 NLT**, *"and when he comes,* **he will convict the world of its sin***, and of God's righteousness, and of the coming judgment."* From this Scripture, we might wonder who or what is the world? It is quite simple, God made (male and female) man in His image to have dominion in this realm (**Genesis 1:26-27**). The world is every domain given to man in the beginning to dominate. However, dominion was lost to the devil through Adam (**Genesis 3**). This was substantiated by a statement of the devil, which was not debunked by Jesus—during His temptation.

Matthew 4:8-10 NLT — *Next the devil took him to the peak of* *a very high mountain and showed him all the kingdoms of the world and their glory. "I will give it all to you," he said, "if you will kneel down and worship me." "Get out of here, Satan," Jesus told him. "For the Scriptures say 'You must worship the Lord your God and serve only him.'"*

The Bible referred to the devil as the ruler of this world (**John 14:30**). The question then becomes if Satan is the ruler of the world, who or what is the Holy Spirit convicting? The answer can be found in Jesus' prayer when He was about to leave the earth (**John 17**). Jesus affirmed that we are in the world, but not of this world. Because we are in this world, our conviction of sin by the Holy Spirit is commensurate with His exposure to our thoughts (as explained in the previous section). He convicts the world around us through us. Therefore, when an unbeliever is in close proximity with a child of God, they feel uncomfortable doing certain things around us. In **Proverbs 16:7 NLT**, the Bible says *"when people's lives please the LORD, even their enemies are at peace with them."* Enjoying peace in the midst of our enemies can be deemed a result of the conviction of the Holy Spirit. When we obey the will of God and live for Him, we will attain great heights. Hence the world will see what is only obtainable through God. In a nutshell, the Holy Spirit enhances us to be effective instruments for God's use in this world. In this way, the salvation work of Jesus puts us right back on top, restoring our God-giving dominion.

He Teaches Us

The purpose of teaching is to bring about knowledge first

and then understanding. This will help a person to apply wisdom when it is needed. The Spirit of God, as we have seen from the names we've discussed earlier, is not just capable of one thing. He is the Spirit of Knowledge, as well as the Spirit of Understanding and Wisdom. This simply means that we can also have these virtues when we get close to the Holy Spirit. Oftentimes, we find it hard to obey, because we do not understand. In other words, we do not know the "*why*." For example, some of us know what we ought to do (i.e. knowledge), and perhaps how to do it (i.e. wisdom), but why we ought to do it remains unknown to us. If we are struggling to obey an instruction or do something, the overarching reason is that we do not understand. As we have learned in Chapter 2, part of the Holy Spirit's assignment in this age is to bring understanding, which will give us the requisite tools to live life to the fullest. The Holy Spirit teaches us by using various methods, some of which include the word of God, spiritual authority and mentorship.

John 14:26 NLT — *But when the Father sends the Advocate as my representative—that is, the Holy Spirit—**he will teach you everything** and will remind you of everything I have told you.*

The promise of teaching is one of the promises of Jesus with regards to the Holy Spirit. God is willing to teach us when we engage Him. *God taught Moses His law and showed all Israel what He could do* (**Psalm 103:7 CEV**). Moses obeyed God and had one of the greatest relationships with God, he was exposed to the "*why*." On the other hand, disobedience was rampant among the Israelites and they had an unstable relationship with God, so, they only knew the "*what*." There is always a lot to learn from the Holy Spirit if we want to. Our desire to be taught by the Holy Spirit is evident in our actions. We ought to consult God through the Holy Spirit before taking any action. It is only then we can apply the right measures to the right situations.

He Advocates for Us

Different translations of the Bible render the importance of the Holy Spirit in **John 14:16** and **John 14:26** using three different words. The New Living translation used advocate, while other translations used either comforter or helper as the variant. If these words were used interchangeably, then there must be a correlation of these words with the description of the Holy Spirit.

According to the dictionary, an advocate is a person who pleads on someone else's behalf or publicly supports their cause. This is so crucial; the devil has deceived many people into believing that God does not like them because they are a mess. Remember, God is love (**1 John 4:8**). Having a Being of God continually pleading for us is genuine love. Hence you are not hated or disliked, you are loved by the maker of all.

The Holy Spirit advocates our cause from the inside out. This is because the spirit realm controls the physical and He is a spirit Being (**Romans 8:16**). Therefore, when a person carries the Holy Spirit every demon in hell knows and stays clear of their spirit. The Holy Spirit, who is pleading our cause in the spirit can also do that in the physical if we allow His flow towards our outer being (i.e., through our soul to our body).

Romans 8:14 NLT — *For all who are led by the Spirit of God are children of God.*

John 3:8 NLT — *The wind blows wherever it wants. Just as you can hear the wind but can't tell where it comes from or where it is going, so you can't explain how people are born of the Spirit.*

We are bound for greatness, both in the physical and the spiritual. Hence no evil shall before us, and **Psalm 23** and **Psalm 91** will be fulfilled in our lives.

The word helper works, because the Holy Spirit pledges His support to our cause. In **Romans 8:26 NLT**, the scripture tells us *"And the Holy Spirit helps us in our weakness. For example, we don't know what God wants us to pray for. But the Holy Spirit prays for us with groanings that cannot be expressed in words."* We can see the Holy Spirit advance our cause by helping us to pray for the right things.

Comfort which means to encourage or console is another work of the Holy Spirit. God put Him here on earth to fill the void of Jesus' physical absence. His ability to search all things (**1 Corinthians 2:10**) makes Him the perfect one to help us through life's hardest challenges. He knows the will of God for our lives, He knows you are not a failure and that God loves you dearly. So, when the enemy comes to attack, He consoles and encourages us with the truth.

Isaiah 59:19b NKJV — *When the enemy comes in like a flood, The Spirit of the LORD will lift up a standard against him.*

The Holy Spirit in the Old Tabernacle

In understanding the Holy Spirit, it is important to dive into some of His experiences. There is a revelation that was revealed in the old testament that will aid our understanding of who the Holy Spirit is. This will be explained briefly; however, it will be sufficient to give the relevant insight.

There are a few numerical numbers that are significant in the Bible. For example, the number seven often means completion. This is synonymous with the fact that, even though God finished the work of creation in six days, He rested on the seventh day. This signifies His confidence in the completion of His creation **(Genesis 1:31)**. Earlier in this chapter, when we discussed the seven spirits of God, we also learned about the significance of the number seven. The number three is also another significant number. This is known to represent wholeness. This was derived from the triune nature of God. Hence when the Bible says *"God made man in His image,"* this was one of many things the Bible was referring to **(Genesis 1:27)**. Just as God is God the Father, God the Son and God the Holy Spirit, man is also a triune being—Man-the Spirit, Man-the Soul and Man-the Body. Therefore, any time we see the number three in the word of God, it is often synonymous with the triune nature of God.

Now, in explaining the God of this age and His significance, let us use one of the examples that involve the number three. The tabernacle that God instructed Moses about in the books of Exodus and Leviticus consisted of three places—the outer court, the holy place and the holy of holies. Relating this to God's salvation work through Jesus, we see that the outer court is the representation of Jesus Christ (the Son), the holy place is the representation of the Holy Spirit, and the holy of holies is the representation of God (the Father). When things are given by God in threes, the revelation behind it often stems from the triune nature of God; this was confirmed in **Hebrews 8:5**. However, in this day and age, we worship God in the Spirit through the God of this age—the Holy Spirit (**John 4:24**).

Hebrews 8:5 NLT — *They serve in a system of worship that is only a copy, a shadow of the real one in heaven. For when Moses was getting ready to build the Tabernacle, God gave him this warning: "Be sure that you make everything according to the pattern I have shown you here on the mountain."*

John 4:24 NLT — *For God is Spirit, so those who worship him must worship in spirit and in truth.*

The allowance and movements in these three places resonate with its classification. For example, there is no restriction to who can come to the outer court; this was and still is the same for Jesus. In **Matthew 9:10 NLT,** the Bible recorded that *"Matthew invited Jesus and his disciples to his home as dinner guests, along with many tax collectors and other disreputable sinners."* In regards to the layout of the tabernacle, Jesus is the outer court. The altar of burnt offerings was situated in the outer court (**Exodus 27:1** and **Leviticus 4:18**); this was where the blood of animals was shed for the remission of sin (**Hebrews 9:22**). So also did Jesus shed His blood for the remission of our sins (**Ephesians 1:7**).

Now, back to our focus in this book—the Holy place (or the inner court). In this age, this is typified by the Holy Spirit, as our tabernacle of worship. In the old tabernacle, only the priests could enter the Holy Place after they had washed their hands and feet with water in the bronze laver (**Exodus 30:17-20**). This was another significant work of Jesus (**1 John 1:9**). As we go through the outer court, we become priests (**1 Peter 2:9**) and are cleansed (**1 John 1:7**). As such, we can enter the Holy place. This simply means, we cannot receive the Holy Spirit until we have confessed and believed Jesus as our personal Lord and savior (**Romans 10:9-10**); this will be discussed in the next chapter.

Furthermore, only the priests had the permission level to access the Holy Place. Their job duty in the Holy Place was to perform sacrifices for the remission of the peoples' sins. However, they all had to go through security screening before entering the Holy Place—cleansing themselves with water. What is the interpretation of this today? When Apostle Peter was writing to the believers under the inspiration of the Holy Spirit, he called us priests (**1 Peter 2:9**). This simply means that the moment we come into Jesus (the outer court), we become priests and gain security clearance into the Holy Place. This is a privilege that the people of Israel didn't have at that time; it was only exclusive to the tribe of Levi (Aaron and his sons). However, we get to enjoy that privilege in this age (**John 1:12**). Also, as a priest in the Holy Place, one major assignment is seen in the statement of Jesus in **Mark 16:15**. To go into the world and make disciples of all. This is our priestly duty today in the Holy Place. As the priests of old sacrifice on behalf of all Israelites, we intercede in prayer and preach the gospel to all today.

1 Peter 2:9 NLT — *But you are not like that, for you are a chosen people. You are royal priests, a holy nation, God's very own possession. As a result, you can show others the goodness of God, for he called you out of darkness into his wonderful light.*

John 1:12 NLT, Emphasis added — *To all who believed him and accepted him, he gave the right to become children of God—priests.*

In the old tabernacle, the Holy place consisted of three significant things (**Exodus 40:22-31**), which connoted three major works of the Holy Spirit in this age. We will explore the three major works of the Holy Spirit next.

The Table of Showbread
(Leviticus 24:5-9, Exodus 25:23-30 & 26:35)

This table was used to display baked bread in the presence of God. This bread was meant to be eaten by only the priests. Therefore, only those who had access to the Holy Place (Inner Court) could eat the bread. As we established earlier, the Holy Spirit is the Holy Place in this day and age. As per **1 Peter 2:9**, salvation through Jesus made us Priests and gave us access to the Holy Place.

In **John 6:35**, Jesus declared that He is the bread of life. **John 1:14** said the word became flesh and dwelled among us. This signifies the word of God spoken to Mary, through the angel in **Luke 1:31**, this word led to the pregnancy that brought about Jesus. Therefore, if Jesus is the word of God and also the bread of life, this means that the word of God is the bread of life. This was why the prayer that Jesus taught his disciples in **Matthew 6:9-13** says, *"give us this day our daily bread."* In other words, give us the word of God needed for the day.

From the tabernacle, we know that only the Priests had access to the showbread (i.e., the bread of life) in the Holy Place. And since the Holy Spirit is the Holy Place today, this means we cannot have access to the word of God except through the Holy Spirit. The Holy Spirit envelopes the word of God; the revelation that brings understanding can only be found in the Holy Spirit

John 14:17 NLT — *He is the Holy Spirit, who leads into all truth. The world cannot receive him, because it isn't looking for him and doesn't recognize him. But you know him, because he lives with you now and later will be in you.*

John 14:26 NLT — *But when the Father sends the Advocate as my representative—that is, the Holy Spirit—he will teach you everything and will remind you of everything I have told you.*

John 16:13 NLT — *When the Spirit of truth comes, he will guide you into all truth. He will not speak on his own but will tell you what he has heard. He will tell you about the future.*

The Holy Spirit is the Holy Place, the showbread is the Word of God, and we become priests by the salvation we receive through Jesus. As such, we have access to the word of God in every season for our edification and growth.

The Golden Lampstand
(Exodus 25:31 & Leviticus 24:1-4)

This is another article found in the Holy Place. This is also symbolic because it gives light to the priests whenever they are in the Holy Place performing the rites. David said in **Psalm 119:105 NLT**, *"Your word is a lamp to guide my feet and a light for my path."* And **Psalm 119:130 NLT** tells us that, *"The unfolding of your words gives light; it imparts understanding to the simple."* From these scriptures, it is crystal clear that the word of God does not only bring light, it also imparts understanding. Therefore, the understanding we gain from the word of God is light.

Now that we have established that the word of God (i.e.,

the Showbread) is in the Holy Spirit (i.e., the Holy Place), and the understanding that comes from the Holy Spirit is light. Therefore, the golden lampstand is the understanding we get from the word through the Holy Spirit. It is imperative we realize that every understanding from the Holy Spirit is light. The Spirit knows everything and can give understanding in anything. When understanding comes, it is revelation and hence the illumination. Again, this kind of diverse understanding is only obtainable in the Holy Spirit.

As this golden lampstand is in the Holy Place, so is every understanding needed for all-round success. Such an understanding is strictly reserved for the priests, who have access into the Holy Place (Holy Spirit) through salvation (Jesus) (**John 14:17**). To put this in perspective, the most current significant insights today are as a result of the variation of understanding deduced from some men of old who are in the Holy Place (Such as Isaac Newton, Johannes Kepler, and many more). Some in the outer court took their insight from the Holy Place and built on it. Imagine what is attainable if we can all be in the Holy Place. Every depth of understanding today, can be traced back to the Holy Place.

The Altar of Incense
(Exodus 30:1 & 40:26)

The third thing that was in the Holy Place of the old tabernacle is the altar of incense. On this altar, the priest burned sweet-smelling incense every morning and evening.

In **Revelation 5:8** there was a reference to the incense burning act in heaven. This makes sense because God said the temple was a replica of the perfect one in Heaven (**Hebrews**

8:5). Hence our prayers as priests are the incense burning today.

Revelation 5:8 NLT — *And when he took the scroll, the four living beings and the twenty-four elders fell down before the Lamb. Each one had a harp, and they held gold bowls filled with incense, which are the prayers of God's people.*

Hebrews 8:5 NLT — *They serve in a system of worship that is only a copy, a shadow of the real one in heaven. For when Moses was getting ready to build the Tabernacle, God gave him this warning: "Be sure that you make everything according to the pattern I have shown you here on the mountain."*

This means that we ought to also pray in the Spirit at all times (**Ephesians 6:18**). This can be in the form of tongues (unknown heavenly language or human language) or our own understanding. Whichever the case might be, our prayers must be done in conjunction with the Holy Spirit. The Bible in **James 4:3** NLT says, *"And even when you ask, you don't get it because your motives are all wrong—you want only what will give you pleasure."* This is exactly what happens when we pray without the Holy Spirit's involvement. Many prayers are unanswered because they were offered outside of the Holy Place (i.e., the Holy Spirit). No matter how good an incense might be, if it is not burned in the Holy Place, it will not serve its intended purpose.

If we genuinely pray in the Spirit, there is practically no way it could be done with the wrong motive. This is because *the Holy Spirit helps us in our weakness. For example, we don't know what God wants us to pray for. But the Holy Spirit prays for us with groanings that cannot be expressed in words* (**Romans 8:26 NLT**).

In the new system of this age, we are priests and our prayers are incenses that must be offered in spirit, by the help of the Holy Spirit, who ensures it is done properly to realize the intended result.

The Gifts of the Holy Spirit

God is the giver of good gifts, and as such, He gives good gifts to people (**James 1:5**). The Holy Spirit is the gift that God gave us, the moment we came to Him through Jesus (**Acts 2:38**). As explained earlier, the Holy Spirit is God; therefore, we can expect Him to be a giver of good gifts also. Gifts are things that are given willingly to someone without payment. Oftentimes we neither ask for them nor deserve them, but they are given to us regardless. There are natural gifts given to us by God as part of our creation; these include talents, abilities and so on. However, there are other kinds of gifts that come from the Holy Spirit. For these gifts, you have no say. The giver of the gifts, the Holy Spirit, gives it as He deems fit.

Now let us focus on those gifts that come from the Holy Spirit. To understand the giving mechanism of God, we must understand that God is God of abundance. There are no limits to what He can give. There are many talents and abilities that have been given to believers and unbelievers alike, which leaves one in awe, day after day. Like I noted in my book "The Person You Should Know," we do not cultivate our talents or abilities here on earth, we only discover what God has deposited inside us. Ideally, schools and places of learning should only facilitate the discovery process of our gifts. These gifts are natural to us and are of no repentance (**Ro-**

mans 11:29); this is why natural gifts are not restricted to just believers. However, certain gifts of the Holy Spirit often manifest to the fullest after we have received the Holy Spirit.

Below is a scripture that gives insight into the gifts of the spirit. Let's dive in together.

1 Corinthians 12:4-11 NLT — *There are different kinds of spiritual gifts, but the same Spirit is the source of them all. There are different kinds of service, but we serve the same Lord. God works in different ways, but it is the same God who does the work in all of us. A spiritual gift is given to each of us so we can help each other. To one person the Spirit gives the ability to give wise advice; to another the same Spirit gives a message of special knowledge. The same Spirit gives great faith to another, and to someone else the one Spirit gives the gift of healing. He gives one person the power to perform miracles, and another the ability to prophesy. He gives someone else the ability to discern whether a message is from the Spirit of God or from another spirit. Still another person is given the ability to speak in unknown languages, while another is given the ability to interpret what is being said. It is the one and only Spirit who distributes all these gifts. He alone decides which gift each person should have.*

From the scripture, we have seen different kinds of gifts available to us through the Holy Spirit. There are a couple of things I will like to highlight. First, just as the giver of a gift decides what gift to give a person, so does the Holy Spirit. He alone decides what gifts, out of the variety of gifts to give us. Of course, we can ask God for gifts (**Matthew 7:7**), desire certain gifts (**Psalm 37:4**) or even covet gifts (**1 Corinthians 12:31**), but the ultimate decision comes from the giver of gifts—the Holy Spirit. From **1 Corinthians 12:4-11** and **Eph-**

esians 2:11-12, insight is gained on some criteria that the Holy Spirit adopts, when making decisions on gifting. The common themes in every gifting of God are "to help each other, to equip the church, and to build the body of Christ." We see that according to **James 4:3**, no matter how much we ask, desire, or covet a gift if our motives are not aligned with the common themes, we might not receive the gift we desire. The gift of the Holy Spirit is for the Church of Christ. Therefore, a healthy church is expected to display all the gifts of the Spirit, as needed for the work of God.

Now that we know what the gifts are and the reason for them, I would like to address a lingering question you might have; "Why do people living in sin display the gifts of the Holy Spirit?"

The Move of the Holy Spirit

Jesus said in **Matthew 18:20 NKJV**, *"For where two or three are gathered together in My name, I am there in the midst of them"* You might say but God is omnipresent, that is, He is everywhere. In that case, what does the scripture above mean? It is quite simple. Yes, God is everywhere at all times. But He is not engaging everywhere at all times. There are places that God will be, just because He had to be there, and not because He wanted to be there. Hence, He is disengaged. David said, *"If I ascend into heaven, you are there; If I make my bed in hell, behold, you are there"* (**Psalm 139:8 NKJV**). This is an example of God having to be where He doesn't want to be. However, His level of engagement in heaven and hell is quite different.

Anytime the presence of God is engaged, things take a different turn.

God is always in our midst, but the question remains, do we engage Him? What Jesus was really saying in **Matthew 18:20** was, "where two or more people are gathered together in My name (in My name simply means and they engage me), I will be there to grant their heart desires." This of course is my interpretation. We have seen this time and time again, when God moves in the midst of His people, many unexplainable things happen. Therefore, when the saints, that is, children of God gather and engage God, He will be there. After all, He made us a promise in **Jeremiah 33:3 NKJV**, *"Call to Me, and I will answer you, and show you great and mighty things, which you do not know."*

In any good system, when things are done in the right way, it produces the right results. This is also true for the principle of engaging the ever-present presence of God. In our case, as saints, we already have one part going good for us; God wants to be in our midst because we are His children (**Psalm 22:3**). The second part is that we have to engage Him. Knowing someone and engaging the person are two different things. For example, the scripture I earlier alluded to in **Jeremiah 33:3 NKJV** is self-explanatory. It tells us that if we want to see great and mighty things we do not know, we must call unto God. Among others, prayer, worship and thanksgiving are some ways that God can be engaged in the gathering of saints.

In this day and age, the God that we engage is the God of this age—the Holy Spirit. There is a common phenomenon that happens when we engage the Holy Spirit; every genuine gift of His is engaged. These gifts are ready to be used by Him. We have seen this over and over again from the scriptures in the new testament. In **Acts 2:4 NLT**, after the disciples engage the Holy Spirit, *"everyone present was filled with the Holy Spirit and began **speaking in other languages**, as the Holy Spirit gave them this ability."* Speaking in another tongue is a gift of the Holy Spirit (**1 Corinthians 12**). Therefore, the move of the Holy Spirit is the display of the gift of the Holy Spirit. When these gifts are displayed, the sole goal is for the edification of the church. Part of what comes with the engagement of the Holy Spirit is that we may receive new gifts if we so desire it (**1 Corinthians 12:31**). However, we don't lose our current gifts, which are put to work to display the power of God. This display of gifts is only meant for God's glory (**1 Corinthians 10:31**). If our intent contravenes this, there is a great likelihood that the Holy Spirit won't be involved. The ever-presence is converted into the anointing when we engage the Holy Spirit.

God works through us, but oftentimes God's medium of flow is through the gifts of the Holy Spirit. I cannot help but stress this fact again; the gifts are for the ***edification*** of the Church. This is important because many think if a person flows in the gifts, then they must be high up there with God. Not quite true and this I will address soon. The gifts should not be the gauge for our personal spiritual growth. However, a mature person will carefully use the gifts in a more appropriate way than a child would. Therefore, the display and quality of gifts are more valuable in the life of a mature Christian. We must understand that gifts are for all. This means that once God's presence is triggered or engaged by a minimum of two or three followers of Christ (**Matthew 18:20**), even if an unbeliever is within that gathering, they will still experience the move of God. In that moment, God can flow to every nuke and cranny through the gift of the Holy Spirit. Hence an unbeliever can get healed in an evangelistic crusade. However, miracles from God can only be retained or sustained by the acceptance of Jesus as the Lord and Savior (**Matthew 12:43-45**).

Let us examine **Acts 2:1-2 NLT.** There are a few things here; first, the believers were gathered in one place. What were they doing? They were there to engage the presence of God. Suddenly, something happened—the move of God.

Acts 2:1-2 NLT — *On the day of Pentecost all the believers were meeting together in one place. Suddenly, there was a sound from heaven like the roaring of a mighty windstorm, and it filled the house where they were sitting.*

When you engage God, He moves in. The moment He moves in, gifts are given and activated as He deems fit, for what He intends to do. In this manner, no one can really escape the wind. When there is a flood, everything in its path gets wet.

Only believers can activate the presence of God; unbelievers can only enjoy the move of God. As I have said before, the blessings received through this medium is only sustained through salvation (i.e., accepting Jesus per **Romans 10:9-10**). Therefore, altar calls are opportunities for unbelievers to surrender their lives to Jesus, before or after such moves of God. This is so because *our great enemy, the devil, prowls around like a roaring lion, looking for someone to devour* (**1 Peter 5:8 NLT**). Also, *"When an evil spirit leaves a person, it goes into the desert, searching for rest. But when it finds none, it says, 'I will return to* *the person I came from.' So, it returns and finds that its former home is all swept and in order. Then the spirit finds seven other spirits more evil than itself, and they all enter the person and live there. And so that person is worse off than before."* (**Luke 11:24-26 NLT**). Hence any blessing or freedom received from God that is not cemented in Him is bound to be lost or stolen.

The Fruit of the Holy Spirit

You can identify them by their fruit, that is, by the way they act. Can you pick grapes from thorn bushes, or figs from thistles? (**Matthew 7:16 NLT**)

The scripture above is simply saying, if we want to recognize what kind of fruit a person carries or produces, their actions say it all. Yes, Jesus was referring to humans here. However, we are in God's image (**Genesis 1:27**), that is, we are spirit beings. I will take this even further by saying, every spirit being can be recognized by their fruit. When the Bible encourages us in **1 John 4:1** to test all spirits, we are simply commanded to examine the kinds of fruit produced by the spirit. Therefore, the fruit of the Spirit listed in **Galatians 5:22-23** is the identifier of the Holy Spirit. Wherever the fruit of the Holy Spirit is absent, He is not there.

We know that fruits are predominantly produced on the branch of a tree (**John 15:4**). Likewise, our actions are our fruit, and the nature of our fruit is dependent on the nature of the tree. Actions are the results of our thoughts, because *as we think in our heart, so are we* (**Proverbs 23:7**). The thoughts we produce are seen by God (**Jeremiah 17:10**). I am not talking about the devil's mind game with the corrupt thoughts he attempts to infuse into our minds. I am referring to our own thoughts, which are products of our meditations. Until we meditate on a certain thought, it is not really ours. This is because only the thought that we meditate on can produce an action. The actions that emanate from our thoughts portray who we are (to people) and the nature of our tree. Therefore, our thoughts reveal who we are to God, while our actions reveal who we are to men.

Due to Adam's sin, we all belong to the tree of evil (**Romans 11:17**). Hence, we needed to be saved through Jesus (**Romans 10:9**), who sanctified us (**Hebrews 10:10**), and regrafted us to the tree of life (**John 15:5 and Romans 11:17**), so that we can produce good fruit in abundance (**John 10:10**). This is why when a person comes to Christ, it is unrealistic to think their actions will change right away. The moment we get saved; this is what happens. We, the branches, are severed from the old tree (the tree of the knowledge of evil **Genesis 2** or the wild olive tree **Romans 11:17**) and grafted to the new tree (the tree of life or olive; **Proverbs 11:30, Genesis 3 and Romans 11:17**). This process may take some time because the branch will have to assimilate the right nutrients before it can produce new fruit for all to see. However, we must keep in mind that in the meantime, the new branch might still have some old fruit on it. Hence some old acts may still pop up, even though the branch is now in Christ. The length of this process depends on the willingness of the branch. Ideally, if we are willing and obedient, the process is faster; and we will live like Jesus in this world—producing the fruit of righteousness from the tree of life (**1 John 4:17**).

Furthermore, we must understand that *a good tree can't pro-*

duce bad fruit, and a bad tree can't produce good fruit (**Matthew 7:18 NLT**). This is the rudiments of the command in **1 John 4:1 NLT**, *"do not believe everyone who claims to speak by the Spirit. You must test them to see if the spirit they have comes from God. For there are many false prophets in the world."* We are meant to identify the tree a person belongs to from the fruit they produce. We cannot afford to be gullible; it is either a person belongs to God or the devil; the way they act is the fruit produced. We are justified to tread carefully based on the fruit. Do you want any part of the fruit in them? If yes, open up to them; if no, take the appropriate steps to protect yourself. People can pretend, but the fruit they produce cannot be hidden, it is practically impossible for an apple tree to produce a grapefruit. This is why we must look beyond what we think and let the consistency of their action speak for itself.

A person with the Spirit of God will produce certain fruits on a consistent basis (**Galatians 5:22-23**). Likewise, a person without the Spirit of God will also produce certain fruits on a consistent basis (**Galatians 5:19-21**). Pretense can be a one-off, but if a person cannot keep up with certain actions, then it is not their true nature. Hence consistency is vital in determining what tree a person belongs to. Our focus is the fruit produced of God. So, what kind of fruit are we talking about? First off, the tree is the tree of life.

Proverbs 11:30 NKJV — *The fruit of the righteous is a tree of life, and he who wins souls is wise.*

This tree was referenced in **Genesis 2:9 & 3:24**. The Bible made us understand that after the first people sinned, God banished them and placed the Cherubim to guard the way to the tree of life. Therefore, the sin of the first people disqualified us from the tree of life and grafted us to the tree of knowledge of good and evil. But to God be the glory, we became righteous through Jesus Christ (**Romans 3:22**). This righteousness reconnected us to the tree of life.

Jesus gave us to the Holy Spirit (**Titus 3:5**). The Holy Spirit is our tree of life today. Now, how is the Holy Spirit the tree of life? and What fruit of the Holy Spirit is produced through us?

The answer to the question is found in **Galatians 5:23-24 NLT**, "*But the Holy Spirit produces this kind of fruit in our lives: **love, joy, peace, patience, kindness, goodness, faithfulness, gentleness, and self-control.*" There is no law against these things!*" In other words, the Holy Spirit and those filled with the Holy Spirit will act out the listed fruit.

There is one important thing that must be discussed before we proceed. As explained earlier, the Bible used "fruit" instead of "fruits" for the nine that were mentioned. This was done consistently across Bible translations. Hence it is not a grammatical error. The Spirit of God is one Spirit and as such one tree—the tree of life. As briefly explained earlier, this tree was first mentioned in the Garden of Eden when Adam and Eve were cast out (**Genesis 3:24**). They were restricted because they sinned, and consequently unentitled to the fruit of the tree anymore. But as children of God, through Jesus, we have been restored and the fruit of this tree is our divine entitlement (**2 Timothy 1:9 & John 1:12**). However, the problem is that we do not know where the physical garden of Eden is located today. Even if we did, there are Cherubim guarding the way to the tree of life (**Genesis 3:24**). Here is the fact, the ultimate tree of life is God, the maker of all life. The physical tree in the garden was only a representation. The same way the Ark of the Covenant was a representation of His presence in the days of the old covenant. Today, we are the walking ark of God's covenant, the carriers of His presence through the Holy Spirit (**1 Corinthians 6:19**). Therefore, the moment we were restored through Jesus, our access was restored to the tree of life—God through the Holy Spirit. Because the Holy Spirit is the God of this age, He is, therefore, the tree of life today.

On a given tree, there is only one kind of fruit; however, in the fruit, there can be many seeds. In the same manner, the nine attributes in **Galatians 5:22-23**, I classify as the seeds of the fruit of the Holy Spirit. Expatiating further, we can say the fruit produced from the tree of life is abundant life (**John 10:10**). The seeds of abundant life are **love, joy, peace, patience, kindness, goodness, faithfulness, gentleness, and self-control**. **John 10:10 NLT** validates this insight; Jesus said, *"The thief's purpose is to steal and kill and destroy. My purpose is to give them a rich and satisfying life."* Another translation says *"that you may have life and have it in abundance."* As established, Jesus gave us access to the Holy Spirit who is the tree of life. An apple tree produces apples as its fruit; likewise, the tree of life produces life as its fruit—a rich and satisfying life. Since seeds are within the fruit, the Bible, in a like manner, provided the composition of the fruit in **Galatian 5:22-23**. Therefore, a rich and satisfying life is a life with all-round success. That is, a healthy person must have all the seeds of the fruit of the Holy Spirit.

In summary, the tree of the Spirit is the tree of life. The tree of life produces the fruit of life. The fruit of the Spirit gives a rich and satisfying life. Because the Spirit gives life

(**John 6:63**). In the fruit of the Spirit, there are a few seeds, which we will dissect next. A rich and satisfying life can only be achieved through faith in Jesus, the author and finisher of our faith (**Hebrews 12:2**). As we dissect each seed, we will see how each one gets us to the destination of abundant life.

Love

As we may know, for every good thing that God gives, the devil replicates its fake. This is one of the seeds of the Holy Spirit that has been bastardized today. When you say "love," many perverted and despicable things come into people's minds. Many atrocities have been done in the name of love. But we are discussing the real meaning of love, from the one who is love—God. So, what is love from God's point of view?

The Bible in **1 John 4:8 NLT** says, *"but anyone who does not love does not know God, for God is love."* This is a very simple and straightforward definition. Any things that cannot be found in God cannot be love. It might look like it, but if it cannot be attributed to God, it is not love. Marriage, which is an institution of love, was God's design. When marriage is done right with God, love reigns and things are different. The family, produced out of marriage, is another example of love God designed. The church of God was created and birthed out of love. When you go to a church where God is resident, you will feel, see, and experience love. In everything that is of God, love is evident and love prevails. Hence everything God is love.

Because God is love, we have to understand genuine love from the lens of God. We learned in our previous discussions that God is triune in nature. Therefore, if God is love and God is triune, then true love is also triune.

Matthew 22:37-39 NLT — *Jesus replied, "'You must* **love the Lord your God** *with all your heart, all your soul, and all your mind.' This is the first and greatest commandment. A second is equally important:* **'Love your neighbor as yourself.**'"

From this scripture, we can see the three dimensions of genuine love. These include love God, love yourselves and love your neighbors.

Love God

In **John 14:15 NLT**, Jesus said, *"If you love me, obey my commandments."* We can see that loving God with everything entails obeying God in everything. When we obey God, we are bound to have a good and satisfying life. **Isaiah 1:19 NLT** says, *"If you are willing and obedient, you shall eat the good of the land."* Obedience is, therefore, synonymous with having the good of the land—a rich and satisfying life. Samuel said to Saul in **1 Samuel 15:22 NLT**, *"what is more pleasing to the LORD: your burnt offerings and sacrifices or your obedience to his voice? Listen! Obedience is better than sacrifice, and submission is better than offering the fat of rams."*

Obeying God is God's interpretation of true love, therefore, everything we do out of obedience to God is deemed as showing our love for Him. The more we obey, the more God-like we become. This is because we take on the nature of the one that has our ears. When we consistently depend on God, He will always want to dwell with us **(John 14:23)**. We see in the life of Abraham and Job that God trusted them so much, to the point of vouching for them (**Genesis 18:19** and **Job 1:8**). Hence when we say holiness, what we are really saying is to obey God's instruction for our individual lives. Holiness does not necessarily mean perfection. It simply means obeying God's individual and collective instructions to the best of our abilities. And when we fall short, we promptly correct our ways—through the conviction of the Holy Spirit. Genuine love for God is when every fibre of our being is mindful to obey God, regardless of our disposition (such as how we feel) or the situation at hand.

Love Yourself

This is another important part of love. There is a saying that "hurt people hurt people." In the same way, I say lovely people will love people. This all starts with the way we see and view ourselves. In accordance with the command in **Matthew 22:37-39**, loving ourselves is the foundation for loving others. Therefore, you cannot genuinely love your neighbor if you don't love yourself; moreover, loving others more or less than you love yourselves is a sin.

It is easy to love ourselves when we know who we are and see ourselves in the right way, that is, the way God sees us.

Psalm 139:14 NKJV — *I will praise You, **for I am fearfully and wonderfully made**; Marvelous are Your works, and that my soul knows very well.*

1 Peter 2:9 NLT — *You are a chosen people. You are royal priests, a holy nation, God's very own possession. As a result, you can show others the goodness of God, for he called you out of the darkness into his wonderful light.*

Colossians 2:9-10 NLT — *For in Christ lives all the fullness of God in a human body. So, you also are complete through your union with Christ, who is the head over every ruler and authority.*

From these scriptures above, we can understand why the instructions about love came the way it did. It is not just a necessity; we must love God first before we can properly love ourselves (without careening down to self-worship). It is in God that our true love dwells. Remember, God is love. There is no other way to love except through God. It is our love towards God that fuels loving ourselves and loving others. Our love for ourselves must be based on the reflection of God's love for us, and this can only be seen when we love God with everything we've got.

When we love ourselves by the reflection of God's love for us, we are insusceptible to pride. This is because our love for ourselves gives glory back to God, and this takes humility to do so. When we are not prideful, God will shower us with His grace (**James 4:6**). This is, therefore, an open door to abundant life, because we are reflecting God's love for our lives. This will eventually overflow to the way we treat others, as we will see next.

Love Your Neighbor as Yourself

As I alluded to earlier, the kind of love we have for ourselves should dictate how we love others. Any deviation from this is a sin. Your neighbor is every other person on earth (**Luke 10:25-37**) that God created; as such, they must be treated with the love that reflects our own love for ourselves.

God is the master creator; He wants us to love our neighbors. Many of us are already living this out without knowing. But the issue is that some do not love God in the way He specified. Here is the right process to all this. First, we love God genuinely, that is, coming to God through Jesus and obeying all His commands to the best of our abilities (**John 14:15**). Then, we love ourselves from the light of God's love, that is, reflecting God's love for us. Subsequently, we can then reflect that same love on others, that is, seeing others the way God sees them. God loves all His creations dearly and wants every one of them to be saved (**John 3:16** and **1 Timothy 2:4**). Hence, we must treat, respect and honor them as God's creations, whether male, female, adult or children. When our love for God is absent, the other two aspects of love will be misaligned. For example, people who hate themselves will hate others; people who are afraid will project their fears on others; people with corrupt intentions will think everyone is out to get them; people who lie will think everyone is lying to them and about them. This is simply because, under normal circumstances, we are wired to love others just the way we love ourselves (**Titus 1:15**).

The kind of love we've just discussed is the way to please God. Every other thing will fall into place when we love in the way God has outlined. Everyone has the tendency to respond positively to genuine and true love (that is, a love that is rooted in the foundation of loving God first). Therefore, *when a man's ways please the LORD, He makes even his enemies to be at peace with him* (**Proverbs 16:7 NKJV**). What other kinds of life would we rather have other than this? One of the ways in which abundant life is evident is when our enemies are at peace with us. Why will our enemies be at peace with us? God made them, and when we show them the reflection of God's love (**Romans 12:20**), they are obliged to reciprocate by being at peace with us.

Joy

This is an interesting one because there are lots of misconceptions about it. The dictionary defines joy as "a feeling of great pleasure and happiness;" however, this is the world's kind of joy. Joy is neither the state of being happy nor the feeling of happiness. Happiness is synonymous with happenings (i.e., events); that is, you are happy when certain events occur. However, joy is not driven by happenings (or events).

Joy is the perpetual state of mind regardless of what has happened, what is happening, or what will happen. You might say we live in a world where bad things often happen; how are we going to dwell in perpetual joy? Remember, joy is a seed in the fruit of the Holy Spirit (**Galatians 5:22**). Hence joy did not originate on earth, neither can it be found on earth; it is of the supernatural. People who have joy are not bothered about the economy or the state of this world (**John 17:16**). We are in Christ (**Romans 8:1**) who is seated far above and beyond what is known or seen by mere humans (**Ephesians 1:21-23**). Now, let's drill even deeper.

Proverbs 15:13 AMP — *A heart full of joy and goodness makes a cheerful face, but when a heart is full of sadness the spirit is crushed.*

Proverbs 17:22 ESV — *A joyful heart is good medicine, but a crushed spirit dries up the bones.*

From these two scriptures, we see that the nature of joy is centrifugal (inward to outward). We can see that we have abundant life and good health when we live in the joy produced by the Spirit of God. The Bible further elucidated when it said, *"do not grieve, for the joy of the Lord is your strength"* (**Nehemiah 8:10b**). The virtue of joy has also been validated by medical science, which predicates living in constant joy as an avenue to keep sickness at bay. This is why when the devil wants to attack a person, he takes away their joy first, throws them into darkness and hits them with sickness. This understanding was what triggered David's prayer in **Psalm 51:12 NLT**, *"restore to me the joy of your salvation, and make me willing to obey you."* For this same reason, when a person comes to Jesus, one of the first things that are restored is joy. They promptly experience the joy of salvation. All genuine children of God must have this with them always. If this is missing, then we are either in sin and haven't amended our ways or we are not saved at all.

This joy is always present in the presence of God; therefore, it is impossible for God to be sick. Also, wherever God is, you will experience this joy. This is one of the pieces of evidence of God's presence in a place. The Bible confirms this in **Psalm 16:11 NKJV**.

"you will show me the path of life; ***In Your presence is fullness of joy****; At Your right hand are pleasures forevermore."*

So, we see that to live in perpetual joy, we must have the presence of God in and around us at all times. This is what we get when the Holy Spirit dwells in us (**Romans 8:11** and **1 Corinthians 6:19**).

Peace

One of the trademarks of our God is peace. This is why the

phrases peace be unto you, peace be still, and many more were used by Jesus during His days on earth. In all scenarios, wherever the presence of God is (for anything other than judgment), you will find His peace there.

Peace is not the absence of trouble; it is the presence of the God of Peace. Thereby, giving us the grace to remain calm even in the face of trouble. Our connection with the God of Peace gives us the grace to stay calm in the face of trouble. Jesus' action in **Mark 4:39** was because He understood what He had and the disciples had no idea. Peace is a supernatural phenomenon. Jesus confirms this in **John 16:33 NLT** when He said, *"I have told you all this so that you may have peace in me. Here on earth, you will have many trials and sorrows. But take heart, because I have overcome the world."*

Peace is domiciled in the presence of God. Furthermore, every instruction or word spoken by God is always accompanied by peace. The peace that accompanies God's word is second to none. The Holy Spirit is the Spirit of Peace, and He is always in agreement with God. Hence, when the heart is troubled and God speaks, peace is restored. Peace is one of the virtues that the devil can neither fake perfectly nor consistently. Unfortunately, his deceit still draws away the attention of many from the God of Peace and the word of God.

It is crucial to state that what we focus on dominates us. When we focus on the capabilities of the God of Peace, His word or His acts, we experience unprecedented peace. Therefore, *be anxious for nothing, but in everything by prayer and supplication, with thanksgiving, let your requests be made known to God; and the* **peace of God**, *which surpasses all understanding, will guard your hearts and minds through Christ Jesus.* (**Philippians**

4:6-7 NKJV). However, if we gaze at the problem, we will experience severe turbulence and anxiety (**Matthew 14:30**).

So far, we have discussed the peace that directly comes from God. However, I would like us to revisit an interesting scripture again. In **Proverbs 16:7 NLT**, the Bible says *"when people's lives please the LORD, even their enemies are at peace with them."* We may ask, I thought peace is a phenomenon with God? How will my enemy be at peace with me? Peace comes from God. However, when we please the God of peace, His peace spreads to everything in us and around us—both living and nonliving. This makes it possible for us to remain in the peace of God and follow peace with all (**Hebrews 12:14** and **Romans 12:18**). When everything around us (including our enemies) is affected by this peace, we will have a good life in abundance, as promised.

Patience

This is often referred to as long-suffering. It is one of many attributes of God that the Holy Spirit passes down to us. The Bible made us understand in **Psalm 136**, that the mercies of the Lord endure forever; therefore, when we were still sinners, Christ died for us (**Romans 5:8**). Hence God's desire is for *everyone to be saved and understand the truth* (**1 Timothy 2:4**). This is the basis for His patience.

Romans 5:3-5 AMP — *And not only this, but [with joy] let us exult in our sufferings and rejoice in our hardships, knowing that hardship (distress, pressure, trouble) produces patient endurance; and endurance, proven character (spiritual maturity); and proven character, hope and confident assurance [of eternal salvation]. Such hope [in God's promises] never disappoints us, because God's love* *has been abundantly poured out within our hearts through the Holy Spirit who was given to us.*

The scripture above gives us insight into patience. Patience is the ability to endure, remain steadfast, immovable and unshakable. All through the scriptures, we see the display of this in God. Hope, which we receive from our salvation in Jesus (**1 Peter 1:3** and **Colossians 1:27**), is the outcome of patience. Patience builds strength and strength builds hope. When we are patient enough to see the outcome of a thing, it builds our faith in God. So, we can see that out of patience comes our ability to see the invisible (**Hebrews 11:27**). The invisible that we are able to see is our confidence and hope of salvation (**Ephesians 2:8-10**). As it is written in **Psalm 30:5b NLT,** "*Weeping may last through the night, but joy comes with the morning.*" If we can stand our ground through the night, we will see light at the end of the tunnel when the morning comes. All this is only possible through Jesus, who gives us access to the Holy Spirit. When we have Him, no situation, trouble or problem can make us impatient or anxious. We know that God *will cause everything to work together for our good, because we love God and we are called according to His purpose* (**Romans 8:28**).

Though, patience is the act of being calm while waiting for what we desire. It is still important to be patient with the right motive if we want to reap the rewards outlined in **Romans 5:3-5**. For example, many people wait primarily because there is no other alternative to achieve their goal. But as children of God, the purpose of our waiting is to exercise, build and strengthen our faith in God. Anything out of this scope is not godly patience. In accordance with **Romans 5:3-5**, every situation we face is an opportunity to build our faith in God. Hence problems are ingredients for building our faith and thereby giving us a tool for an abundant life.

Kindness

All that is to be known about kindness is summarized in **Ephesian 4:32 NLT**, *"Instead, be **kind** to each other, tender-hearted, forgiving one another, just as God through Christ has forgiven you."* Using the systematic logic of biblical interpretation, the latter is often an expansion of the former. In this case, when we are kind, we will become tender-hearted. Then, when we are kind and tender-hearted, we will forgive one another. Therefore, without kindness, we cannot forgive one another; consequently, we will be violating the condition for our own forgiveness in **Matthew 6:14**. As per the dictionary, being kind means a lot of things, such as caring, compassion et al. However, in accordance with the Bible, we see that the theme of kindness is to forgive one another. If we are compassionate towards others, we will forgive them regardless of what was done. Forgiving someone takes the grace of God and the help from the Holy Spirit, who does this on a regular basis. The Bible tells us that it was the kindness of God that let Him forgive us through Jesus. So, we are forgiven through Jesus, because of the kindness of God.

You may wonder, but why is this a part of the fruit of the Holy Spirit? In **Ephesian 4:31** and **Galatians 5:19-21,** we see the product of our nature. In these scriptures, it is very clear that being kind is not part of our nature. But kindness is the nature of God. We are not capable of producing kindness consistently without the help of God, through the Holy Spirit.

Being kind means forgiving others and being tender-hearted, regardless of what was done. This is indeed difficult because the devil is in this realm (**2 Corinthians 4:4**). He makes it very difficult to exercise this nature of God. Notwithstanding, with the help of the Holy Spirit, we are more than conquerors (**Romans 8:37**).

Goodness

Goodness is the act of being good. This simply means we must be good. However, according to **Mark 10:18**, Jesus asked the young rich man *"Why do you call me good? Only God is truly good."* Jesus refuted the fact that He is good and said only God is truly good. This is significant because if God wants us to be good, why then did Jesus say only God is truly good? Jesus simply indicated that there was no goodness in our nature, and any form of goodness came from only God. We may say well, according to **Genesis 1:31**, everything God created was good; we are His creation; hence we are good, aren't we? Yes, we are created in God's image and we were good at the beginning (**Genesis 1**). But sin corrupted our God-given good nature and made it bad (**Genesis 3**). However, in the New Testament, the salvation work of Jesus restored us back to the good nature through the Holy Spirit. God still wants us to be good and this was why He sent Jesus. In **Mark 10:18**, Jesus was calling the attention of the rich young man to this. All goodness comes from God, and if we want to be good again, we must run back to God.

The dictionary describes goodness as *"the quality of being morally good or virtuous."* This is so accurate; goodness can be summarized as being righteous.

2 Corinthians 5:21 NLT, emphasis added — *for God made Christ, who never sinned, to be the offering for our sin, so that we could be made right (morally good or virtuous) with God through Christ.*

Hence the acts and results of goodness are the fruit of the Spirit because it is a result of our faith in God through Jesus Christ. It was Jesus who gave us access to the Holy Spirit. This is validated in **Romans 3:22 NLT**, *"We are made right with God by placing our faith in Jesus Christ. And this is true for everyone who believes, no matter who we are."*

We must be people of integrity (**Matthew 5:37**) to exude goodness. Unfortunately, goodness is a scarce virtue in today's world; in spite of its innumerable benefits. Pursuing goodness puts you under God's divine protection (**1 Peter 3:13**).

Faithfulness

All through the Bible, we see this attribute of God over and over again. But what exactly is faithfulness? In a very simple term, it is the act of being faithful. To break this down even further, the etymology of the word "faithful" reveals that it is composed of two words "faith and full," which means full of faith. The antonym of the word faithful is faithless (i.e., lack of faith). So, what is faith and why do we have to be full of it?

In accordance with **Hebrews 11:1 ISV**, *"faith is the assurance that what we hope for will come about and the certainty that what we cannot see exists."* Faith simply means to be steady in our belief, that is, to be steadfast, immovable and reliable. In **Genesis 18:19**, God vouched for Abraham that he will teach his house God's precepts. This meant that God could rely on

Abraham. God is faithful because He is Jehovah Shammah (the Lord is there); He is always there for His people. When you are facing a challenge, what is your first resort? Do you seek God's help or are you trying to figure it out yourself? Praying to God is an act of faith, it means we are putting our faith in God; hence we are there when we need Him or when He needs us. Therefore, faithfulness is our being available when God needs us and God's availability when we need Him.

Matthew 6:33 NLT — *Seek the Kingdom of God above all else, and live righteously, and he will give you everything you need.*

Jeremiah 33:3 NKJV — *Call to Me, and I will answer you, and show you great and mighty things, which you do not know.*

Matthew 6:33 is God instructing us to be available when He needs us; **Jeremiah 33:3** is God assuring us that He will be available when we need Him. We can see that faithfulness is a two-edged sword and both edges tie us directly back to God, and as such, we cannot be faithful without the help of the Holy Spirit.

Gentleness

One of the ways to preserve our salvation is gentleness. This is because the Holy Spirit is a gentle Spirit. The Bible shows us this nature of God in **Revelations 3:20 NLT,** *"Look! I stand at the door and knock. If you hear my voice and open the door, I will come in, and we will share a meal together as friends."*

Gentleness is one of the ways to distinguish the kind of spirit at work. For example, when the Holy Spirit is in a person, He connects with their spirit (**Romans 8:16**). However, it is only if we allow Him that He begins to flow, from our spirit into other parts of our being. Therefore, a child of God with the Holy Spirit can still be oppressed by demons in other parts of their beings. This is because they may have limited the flow of the Holy Spirit. On the other hand, when a demon enters a person, either through the spirit or other means, like the madman of Gadara (**Luke 8:36-39**), the demon tries to illicitly take charge of the person's beings without permission. This is why when a person is possessed by a demon, every part of their being is under siege.

The Holy Spirit is the Spirit of God; hence He has the power of God. God made us and He can make us do anything. However, because of His gentle nature, He gave us free will and wants us to choose what we want. Knowing who you are, that is, your capabilities, and bringing that under subjection is the definition of gentleness. Like many others have defined it, it is strength under control. So, for the sake of our free will, the Holy Spirit brought His capabilities under control. Therefore, *the spirits of prophets are subject to prophets* (**1 Corinthians 14:32**).

From this understanding, gentleness for us entails being in full control of the power that we have (i.e., we are not being controlled by the power). Knowing what you have and when to use it is not weakness—it is strength.

We can only commune with God and receive from Him when we are gentle. This is because God will not violate our boundaries. He will never give us what we do not want, need or desire. Revelation is revealed when we can see clearly and understood when we are gentle. The opposite of being gentle is being brutal. A brute will always lord their power over others without fail. Being a brute makes an individual susceptible to the devil's artifice of ignorance, which debilitates them from hearing and receiving from God. Because vacancy is not permitted in the spirit realm, the devil will swoop in and feed the individual with lies that can destroy them.

Another word for gentleness is meekness. This was one of Moses' greatest assets (**Numbers 12:3**) and we are conversant about the high altitude he attained in the flesh. Therefore, I put it to you that you must adopt this nature of God if you want to genuinely walk with Him and to scale greater heights. As a child of God, you know what you have and what you are capable of, hence, you must put power under control. Bring it under the subjection of God. Do only the things that He wants you to do with His power; you will abound in His power and be entrusted with more authority. The meeker and gentler we become, the more authority we are given access to exercise. Just like a signed blank cheque will not be given to an individual that cannot control their appetite for spending. God will never give power or more power to someone who cannot bring that power under control. Therefore, gentleness is one of the ways to receive more valuables from God to aid good life.

Self-Control

This is the seed of the fruit of the Spirit that was listed last and it is really the crown jewel. This is because it seals each and every seed; it is the icing on the cake, the final layer of gladness. Self-control is the ability to control oneself. Looking at the definition of gentleness, which we defined as power under control, we can see that control is present. I call this the crown jewel because if we have each and every other seed we've discussed without self-control, we will get bruised.

It is the devilish nature in humans that compels them to take advantage of others. Our societies have been structured in a manner that encourages exploiting others and stepping on toes to get to the top. Without self-control, we will not only be vulnerable to the exploitation of the devil but to humans as well; we will take advantage of others and others will take advantage of us. The Bible confirms this in **Proverbs 25:28 NLT**, *"A person without self-control is like a city with broken-down walls."* Samson lacked self-control and he lost his power (**Judges 16**), Saul lacked self-control and he lost his kingdom (**1 Samuel 15**), Moses lacked self-control and he didn't enter the promised land (**Deuteronomy 1**), Judas lacked self-control and he lost his place in God (**Matthew 26 & 27**). The point is, everything is at stake when we lack self-control.

Like God, humans are triune in nature (**Genesis 1:27**); hence oneself is referring to all parts of our being—spirit, soul and body. Therefore, self-control is applicable to our spirit, soul and body. As we can imagine, there are different ways to control ourselves. To drill deeper into this, I will encourage you to read "A Discipline Life by Emmanuel Adewusi."

Furthermore, self-control can be defined as a code of conduct. But following this code consistently is a whole different thing entirely. This is the difference between self-control and self-discipline. Control is simply the ability to say yes or no; the ability to stop, pause or continue. It is our mental capacity to know what is right and what is wrong. Discipline on the other hand is the ability to apply control consistently, regardless of the situation. Therefore, the fruit of the Spirit listed in the Bible is only the entrance door; once we get in, numerous pruning activities that will advance us beyond the basics will take place. Remember, *the way of the righteous is like the first gleam of dawn, which shines ever brighter until the full light of day* (**Proverbs 4:18 NLT**).

The Gift Vs the Fruit

There is a myth going around today. This is what made this subtopic very important. Many think that once a person flows in the gift of the Holy Spirit, they are high up there with God. This might be true, but it is not always the case.

Recently, I had a chat with my wife about this particular subject. She said, from her understanding, the difference between both of them was: "the gift of the Spirit is given, but the fruit of the Spirit must be cultivated." This is absolutely true! When a person gives you a gift, all you have to do is accept it; the choice on the usage of the gift is ultimately yours to make. The Bible made us understand in **1 Corinthians 12:11 NLT** that, "*It is the one and only Spirit who distributes all these gifts. He alone decides which gift each person should have.*" Therefore, the giving of the gift and the type of gift we receive is determined by the Holy Spirit. Also, our qualification for the gifts is determined by the Holy Spirit.

On the other hand, the fruit in the sense that everything listed in **Galatians 5:22-23** is just the starting point. The moment we become born again and receive the Holy Spirit, we have access to the fruit. However, it can lay dormant if we do not cultivate it. As earlier alluded to, the list in the scripture for the fruit of the Spirit is singular. This means once we have the Holy Spirit, the fruit that carries all the seeds noted in the scripture (**Galatians 5:22-23**) is within us, and can be activated. Also, we've discussed that there is a difference between self-control and self-discipline. We can say self-control is the starting point, while self-discipline is the end result. Eventually, the goal is for us to have self-discipline, even though it wasn't listed in **Galatians 5**. We are to keep increasing in the fruit of the Spirit until we become perfect (**Matthew 5:48**). We are to keep loving until it is impossible to be ensnared by offence. Absolute love doesn't start overnight; it is the work of the Holy Spirit to keep cultivating us. We are to be Joyful until we have no room for sadness, in spite of what is going on. Joy must be rooted within us; from our spirit to our soul and out through the body. We must keep growing until we are *perfect, even as our Father in heaven is perfect* (**Matthew 5:48 NLT**). Jesus wants to *present us to himself as a glorious church without a spot or wrinkle or any other blemish—holy and without fault* (**Ephesians 5:27 NLT**). Therefore, until we leave this earth by death or rapture, we must continue to cultivate the fruit with the help of the Holy Spirit, until we are deemed perfect to meet the Father in heaven. But in the meantime, we have access to the Father (**Hebrews 10:19**) through the righteousness of Jesus (**2 Corinthians 5:21**). Therefore, we pray to God and approach Him in the name of the one whose righteousness we are using.

Oftentimes we see people who are not necessarily holy or walking with God perfectly, but they are still flowing in the gift. Why? This is another important contrast between the fruit and the gifts. To be very clear, each and every time the

Bible mentioned the gift, it was accompanied by the statement, *"for the edification of the church."*

Ephesians 4:11-13 NLT— *Now these are the **gifts** Christ gave to the **church**: the apostles, the prophets, the evangelists, and the pastors and teachers. Their **responsibility** is to equip God's people to do his work and **build up the church**, the body of Christ. This will continue until we all come to such unity in our faith and knowledge of God's Son that we will be mature in the Lord, measuring up to the full and complete standard of Christ.*

From this scripture, we know that this is about the fivefold ministry. The purpose is therefore for the church and not for individual gain. This was repeated again in the scripture below.

Romans 12:5-8 NLT — *so it is with Christ's body. We are many parts of one body, and we all belong to each other. In his grace, God has given us different gifts for doing certain things well. So, if God has given you the ability to prophesy, speak out with as much faith as God has given you. If your gift is serving others, serve them well. If you are a teacher, teach well. If your gift is to encourage others, be encouraging. If it is giving, give generously. If God has given you leadership ability, take the responsibility seriously. And if you have a gift for showing kindness to others, do it gladly.*

In this verse, other kinds of gifts are outlined. But the goal here is also not for individual gain, but for the benefit of the body of Christ (i.e., the Church). We are commanded by the Word to do this and that for others. Lastly, let's look at:

1 Corinthians 12:7-11 NLT — *a spiritual **gift** is given to each of us **so we can help each other**. To one person the Spirit gives the ability to give wise advice; to another the same Spirit gives a message of special knowledge. The same Spirit gives great faith to another,* *and to someone else the one Spirit gives the gift of healing. He gives one person the power to perform miracles, and another the ability to prophesy. He gives someone else the ability to discern whether a message is from the Spirit of God or from another spirit. Still another person is given the ability to speak in unknown languages, while another is given the ability to interpret what is being said. It is the one and only Spirit who distributes all these gifts. He alone decides which gift each person should have.*

As we can see, the gifts are not for individual glory, but for the edification and growth of the collective body of Christ. Therefore, we don't get to choose how we will help; the Holy Spirit decides how we can add value to the church. However, we are encouraged to *earnestly desire the most helpful gifts* (**1 Corinthians 12:31**).

Due to the purpose of the gift, anybody can be used for the benefit of the church. Here is why. A healthy church will have the fruit and all the gifts on display, but a healthy individual will have the fruit. Only through the fruit can we engage the presence of God. The gifts are then activated by the presence of God. A person with the gift and without the fruit is unhealthy. If such a person is in close proximity to the engaged presence of God, and their gift is needed, they can be used by God (if they are available) for the benefit of the church. We must understand that there are all kinds of vessels within the church (**2 Timothy 2:20**). It is the fruit that classifies what type of vessel we are. This doesn't change their state of unhealthiness. Hence, we can judge our individual spiritual health by the presence of the fruit of the spirit.

We might be wondering what are the criteria for the gift, in which the Holy Spirit decides who gets what. This is simple. God will not give us more than we have the capacity for (**1 Corinthians 10:13**). Our capacity (i.e., what we can handle) determines what kind of gifts we get (**Matthew 25:14-30**). Our capacity is also ideally rooted in the fruit of the spirit. This is also true for the increment of gifts. Our increased capacity coupled with our stewardship is the determinant. Therefore, the more we increase in the fruit of the spirit, the more our capacity increases, so that we can be further used by God as a vessel unto honor (**2 Timothy 2:20**). For example, the more we love others, the more God can flow from us to them without any kind of hindrance. This is because the gifts are underpinned by trust. Can God trust us? The only way to answer this question is by the fruit we produce.

We noticed that the gift was introduced and discussed in **1 Corinthians 12** by the end of that chapter, we were ushered into the fruit of the Spirit. **1 Corinthians 13** was all about love which is a seed of the fruit of the spirit. Prior to teaching us about love in **1 Corinthians 13**, the Bible said *"but now let me show you a way of life that is best of all"* (**1 Corinthians 12:31**). In other words, we have been discussing what is good; however, let me show you what's better, and then went on to discuss the seed, love. It is imperative to state that when the fruit is lacking, it does not matter whether the gifts are active or inactive, it will be contaminated. Such a person is a muscle for hire. The devil can use them as well as God. It is the fruit that keeps the gifts for God alone, pure and increases it in leaps and bounds.

There is something I want us to consider. Many times, when people with gifts are not living right, that is, the fruit is lacking, they can still flow in their gifts. The Bible tells us that we all naturally have some gifts within us. Jesus gave gifts to men (**Ephesians 4:8**). This is why some people can do certain things out of the ordinary. However, if this is not brought under the subjection of the giver—God, it will be corrupted. When we are in sin (unsaved or backslid state), some of these gifts (the ones received naturally or through salvation) may remain. This is because the *gifts of God and His call will not be withdrawn* (**Romans 11:29**). However, in some instances some may be withdrawn; like Samson in the book of Judges. Whether a gift remains or is withdrawn is solely dependent on the giver—God. Therefore, when a person is living a life that does not please God, they may still operate in the gifts, but it won't be pure and it can easily be hijacked by the devil. However, if we bring our gifts under God through genuine repentance and total surrender, it gives way to the functioning of the Holy Spirit and His fruit.

Another reason why God tends to flow in impure vessels may be due to the deficiency of clean vessels with that gift. This is why the Bible said that we who are genuine *should earnestly desire the most helpful gifts* (**1 Corinthians 12:31 NLT**). We are reminded in the Bible that there are all kinds of vessels in the church.

2 Timothy 2:20 NLT — *In a wealthy home some utensils are made of gold and silver, and some are made of wood and clay. The expensive utensils are used for special occasions, and the cheap ones are for everyday use.*

The wealthy home here is the body of Christ, that is, the Church. The kind of vessel we are is solely dependent on the state of our gifts (i.e., how pure it is). The fruit is what makes us a vessel of honor. Imagine, a genuine child of God comes to church with great anticipation to receive from his Father—God. But the available vessel—the Pastor—is impure. God will have to flow through the impure vessel for the sake of His church. All that God does is for the sake of His church, that is, His people. And as such, He will use any available vessel for the sake of His church. If such an available vessel then appraises themself based on their use by God, they will be mistaken.

In **Matthew 7:23 NLT**, we are privy to what will happen in heaven. Jesus said *"on judgment day many will say to me, 'Lord! Lord! We prophesied in your name and cast out demons in your name and performed many miracles in your name.' But I will reply, 'I never knew you. Get away from me, you who break God's laws.'"* I cringe anytime I read this scripture. There are many interpretations of this scripture. But here is mine. First off, for a person to have the gut to confront Jesus means that they actually did those things in His name. However, I am inclined to believe that these were people that were used by God as available vessels and not necessarily anointed vessels. Genuine children of God are both anointed and available. Anyone that is available and not anointed by God can either be used by God or the devil. These available vessels were not operating in the fruit, but the gifts were activated for the sake of the church. It is important to know that operating in the gifts alone does not make us right with God. The gifts only make us God's servants; it is the fruit that qualifies us His sons and daughters.

Imagine working at your dad's company, you are his child, as well as his employee. Even if you offended him at home, he will still work with you in the office. However, this doesn't mean all is well between both of you. Though the employer-employee relationship is solid, the father-son relationship is strained and must be resolved. The nature of God is the fruit of the Holy Spirit (**1 John 4:8**), and because we are of God, we must exhibit His nature (**Matthew 5:48**). Do not use the gifts to grade your spiritual standing, do so with the fruit.

The Bible said in **Matthew 7:16 NLT**, *"you can identify them by their fruit, that is, by the way they act."* The gift is not the primary criterion for determining the efficacy of our walk with God—it is the fruit. Our spiritual height in God is directly proportional to our increase in the fruit of the Spirit. Hence desire the gifts and keep increasing in the fruit with the help of the Holy Spirit; subsequently, the gifts will come alive. Pursue after the fruit and the gifts will follow. If you pursue after the gifts, you might end up a casualty of deception. There are all sought of gifted fake people out there—false teachers, false prophets, false healing ministers and so forth. However, the fruit of the Holy Spirit cannot be purported. You can fake it, but you cannot do so consistently. It is quite easy to discern.

In conclusion, I would like to reinforce this again. We saw previously that the gifts are for the edification of the body of Christ. The fruit, on the other hand, is for our own edification. Like I have just explained, the fruit is for a rich and satisfying life in abundance, which starts first with us and then spreads to others. However, when we are moved to use the gifts, it is usually not for personal gain, but for the edification of the church. May God help us!

The Baptism of the Holy Spirit

This is one of the most important phenomena that is required of every genuine child of God. Until we are baptized in the Holy Spirit, we neither enjoy our relationship with Him nor operate at the spiritual level we are destined to function. The Bible made us understand that only those *who are led by the Spirit of God are children of God* (**Romans 8:14 NLT**). Baptism is what gives us the certainty that we are being led. What is the baptism of the Holy Spirit?

When we become saved, our spirit is connected to the Holy Spirit. This is the anointing within; as genuine children of God, we all have this (**Romans 8:16**). Therefore, we get convictions right away. Yes, we cannot be possessed, but our soul and body can still be oppressed by the devil. This is why there are some Spirit-filled Christians who are still under the oppression of the devil. Unless our being is swallowed up completely (spirit, soul and body) by the Holy Spirit, the devil can still oppress us. Hence the importance of the baptism of the Holy Spirit.

After breathing on the disciples and giving them the Holy Spirit (**John 20:22**), Jesus told them in **Acts 1:8**: "*But you will receive **power** when the Holy Spirit comes **upon** you. And you will be my witnesses, telling people about me everywhere—in Jerusalem, throughout Judea, in Samaria, and to the ends of the earth.*" Therefore, it is the Holy Spirit upon us (through the baptism) that gives us power to fulfill Jesus' command in **Mark 16:15**. In other words, it is His power that activates and fuels His gifts, which allows the anointing within us to manifest. This was evident in the lives of the disciple all through the book of Acts.

THE MOST IMPORTANT PERSON OF OUR TIME - 135

As they were being filled with the Holy Spirit, the gifts were activated for the salvation of souls. Glory to God! The old testament era mostly operated in the opposite; the anointing came upon, but not necessarily within. Jesus' salvation work mitigated such a phenomenon. Praise God! Now we can have the anointing within, which activates and cultivates the fruit, as well as the anointing upon, which activates the gifts.

Baptism simply means to be infused, swallowed up, or immersed. In this context we can say, it is an immersion or infusion in the Holy Spirit. This is exactly what God had planned for this age.

Acts 2:17 NLT — *"'In the last days,' God says, 'I will pour out my Spirit upon all people. Your sons and daughters will prophesy. Your young men will see visions, and your old men will dream dreams.'"*

God gave us the right expectation for the last days in **Acts 2:17**. As per Jesus' prophecy in **Matthew 24**, we are in the last days. Therefore, we are qualified for the infusion of the Holy Spirit. It is God's plan to pour out His Spirit on all of us. If you are a genuine child of God, it is your right. As said by many servants of God, we are a spirit being with a soul living in a body. As such, until we are infused with the Holy Spirit, we cannot produce the maximum results.

When we are immersed in something, it means we are completely swallowed up in that thing. The moment we receive Jesus, we have the Spirit of Christ inside us (**Romans 8:9**). This simply means we have received the Holy Spirit, but we might not yet be immersed in the Holy Spirit (**Ephesians 1:13-14**). There are cases where we can receive the Holy Spirit and be immersed in the Holy Spirit at the same time—like

Cornelius in **Acts 10**. However, for many, immersion is usually the next phase after salvation. When we are immersed in the Holy Spirit, our entire being (spirit, soul and body) is saturated by Him and under His control. Hence no devil or force of darkness can touch us as long as we obey Him.

After Jesus left the earth, the disciples had to press in for this immersion, as advised by Jesus. As mentioned earlier, the disciple already received the Holy Spirit, but they were not yet immersed in the Holy Spirit (**John 20:22**). The first immersion happened in **Acts 2:1-13 NLT**:

On the day of Pentecost, all the believers were meeting together in one place. Suddenly, there was a sound from heaven like the roaring of a mighty windstorm, and it filled the house where they were sitting. Then, what looked like flames or tongues of fire appeared and settled on each of them. And everyone present was filled with the Holy Spirit and began speaking in other languages, as the Holy Spirit gave them this ability.

At that time there were devout Jews from every nation living in Jerusalem. When they heard the loud noise, everyone came running, and they were bewildered to hear their own languages being spoken by the believers.

They were completely amazed. "How can this be?" they exclaimed. "These people are all from Galilee, and yet we hear them speaking in our own native languages! Here we are—Parthians, Medes, Elamites, people from Mesopotamia, Judea, Cappadocia, Pontus, the province of Asia, Phrygia, Pamphylia, Egypt, and the areas of Libya around Cyrene, visitors from Rome (both Jews and converts to Judaism), Cretans, and Arabs. And we all hear these people speaking in our own languages about the wonderful things

God has done!" They stood there amazed and perplexed. "What can this mean?" they asked each other.

But others in the crowd ridiculed them, saying, "They're just drunk, that's all!"

Prior to this event, the Holy Spirit mostly came upon people. He mainly came upon prophets, priests, kings or seers for the work that God wanted to do at that point in time. However, in this day and age, the Holy Spirit can remain in and upon us for the rest of our lives. That is, we can have the anointing upon and within us for the rest of our days. All thanks to God for Jesus' work of salvation on the cross.

From the scripture above, there are three things I would like to mention.

The first is in **Acts 2:1**, we saw that the disciples were in one place meeting together. Other translations gave more insight that they were in one accord, that is, in alignment and agreement. They were praying earnestly for the Holy Spirit as instructed by their Master—Jesus in **Acts 1**. This simply means, if we are to receive the immersion of the Holy Spirit, we must ask for it (**Matthew 7:7-8**). We must earnestly seek it through prayer. The immersion of the Holy Spirit does not always come automatically, not even to Jesus' first disciples. It comes when we desire and press for it. Oftentimes, it is advisable to seek the help of a higher authority (someone operating in that realm) to pray with us during this quest. In the case of the disciples, they had nobody, since Jesus had already left the earth. But today, we have men and women that God can use for this, so why do it the hard way? One of the many church edification reasons for our local church leadership is this. Remember that even God had to go through Moses to impart

His anointing upon the seventy elders (**Numbers 11:25**). Even though Joshua had the Spirit of God, Moses still had to lay his hands on him as instructed by God, to impart God's anointing upon him (**Numbers 27:18**). Hence you can either immerse yourself or get someone who is already immersed to pull you in. I strongly believe that being pulled in might just be the easy way in. This is the concept behind the laying on of hands (**Numbers 27:18, Acts 8:17** and **Acts 19:6**). There is a transference of spirit when hands are laid.

The second thing we noticed was the answer to their prayer in **Acts 2:2-3**. The Holy Spirit came to impart tongues of fire on their heads. I must be very clear here; this was the method that the Holy Spirit chose to appear here. It doesn't mean that the Holy Spirit will come in this way every time. When it comes to the Holy Spirit, there is no one-size-fits-all. He is God and can choose what way He wants to show up. In fact, in **Luke 3:22**, when Jesus was receiving His own baptism, the Spirit decided to descend on Him like a dove. For many of us He may show up and we start shaking or crying. It is all well and good. Another vital point in these verses is that the fire descended to the top of their head because the head controls the whole body. The one that lays hold of the head has authority over the whole body. Likewise, the descent of the fire upon their heads signifies that their whole body had caught the fire of the Holy Spirit. Hence this is an immersion in the Holy Spirit.

The next observation from this scripture is from **Acts 2:3-13**. We saw the display of the gifts of the Holy Spirit. They spoke in the tongues of men. Everyone in Jerusalem from other nations could hear their language being spoken by the disciples, who had not learned their language. This is the gift of the Holy Spirit. I would like to discuss this further. If we have been around the church, we must have had the phrase *"to receive the Holy Spirit with the evidence of speaking in tongues."* This is an example. But do you always speak in tongues when you receive the immersion of the Holy Spirit?

First, let us look at tongues. Tongues simply mean languages. And contrary to many beliefs, there are two types of languages; the heavenly language and human language (**1 Corinthians 13:1**). The display we saw in **Acts 2** is the human language. The Holy Spirit can give us access to these two languages supernaturally without learning it. I don't think we can even learn the heavenly language if we wanted to. We have heard about occurrences, where missionaries travelled to another country, and spoke the native language to communicate salvation messages, despite not knowing the native language prior. This is an example of the manifestation of the gifts of the Holy Spirit. For human languages, oftentimes, we have people who can understand it—like the case of the disciples. However, the heavenly language is the one that we often need the Spirit to give interpretation (**1 Corinthians 12:28-30**). When Spirit-filled Christians pray in the spirit; the Holy Spirit gives them utterances as seen in **Acts 2:4**.

To answer the question I raised earlier, there is always evidence of speaking in tongues when we receive the baptism of the Holy Spirit. These three scriptural references will validate this conclusion. Because *the facts of every case must be established by the testimony of two or three witnesses* (**2 Corinthians 13:1**). First, when the disciples were baptized, they spoke in tongues (**Acts 2:1-13**). Second, Cornelius and his family received the baptism at the same time they got saved, and they spoke in tongues (**Acts 10:46**). Third, the believers spoke in tongues when they received the baptism of the Holy Spirit (**Acts 19:6**).

Lastly, there is something that must be addressed about the baptism of the Holy Spirit. **Ephesians 5:18 NLT** states, *"Do not to be drunk with wine, because that will ruin your life. Instead, be filled with the Holy Spirit."* This scripture indicates that we must be constantly filled with the Holy Spirit. This implies that the immersion of the Holy Spirit is not a one-time affair. To keep the fire burning, we must continually immerse ourselves in the Holy Spirit. The disciples were immersed in **Acts 2:1-13**, and again in **Acts 4:31**, yet again in **Acts 13:52**. Here are the facts, we come in contact with all kinds of people and demons daily. These contacts, either knowing or unknowing, challenges the anointing upon us on a daily basis. If we examine the story of Elijah, it seems odd that the prophet, who had just called down fire from heaven and killed many prophets of Baal, was on the run by virtue of Jezebel's threat (**1 Kings 18 &19**). As understood from the explanations of my spiritual father, Elijah had exhausted the anointing upon him to call down fire from heaven. Hence the threat from a demonic Jezebel put him to flight. Before that when he was charged, he was doing the taunting. Therefore, we must continually be immersed in the Holy Spirit.

Praying in the Holy Spirit

John 14:26 NKJV says *"But the Helper, the Holy Spirit, whom the Father will send in My name, He will teach you all things, and* *bring to your remembrance all things that I said to you."* In this verse, Jesus qualifies the Holy Spirit as the helper. Here is why. Just as the main mission of Jesus on earth was to restore us back to God, the Holy Spirit is here to help us develop and sustain the salvation we receive through Jesus. He is also here to help us in knowing and getting close to God. In order to do this, the help of the Holy Spirit is available to us in every activity that involves us and God. In fact, it is simply impossible in this day and age to know God, grow in God or receive anything from God without the help of the Holy Spirit.

In **James 4:3 NKJV,** the Bible reveals a reason to us why many prayers are unanswered. It says, *"you ask and do not receive, because you ask amiss, that you may spend it on your pleasures."* It is important to understand that prayer is a form of communion with God. When we pray, we are seeking communion and fellowship with God. Therefore, the act of praying encapsulates a typical act that requires the help of the Holy Spirit. From the scripture above, we know that we are not receiving because we are asking wrongly. Many times, we are unaware of what we need to know spiritually. This is because we are more prone to physical things. Prayer is a spiritual exercise that necessitates spiritual insight into things. Everything that happens in the physical is a finished product of the spiritual. Job's test and trial were sealed in the spiritual world before it was manifested in the physical (**Job 1 & 2**). Based on these facts, it is very clear that we need the help of the Holy Spirit in our prayers.

Romans 8:26-27 NLT — *And the Holy Spirit helps us in our weakness. For example, we don't know what God wants us to pray for. But the Holy Spirit prays for us with groanings that cannot* be expressed in words. And the Father who knows all hearts knows what the Spirit is saying, for the Spirit pleads for us believers in harmony with God's own will.

1 Corinthians 2:10 NLT — *But the Helper, the Holy Spirit, whom the Father will send in My name, He will teach you all things, and bring to your remembrance all things that I said to you.*

He helps us to pray the right prayers with the right motives so that we get the right answers from God. Glory to God!

Praying in the Holy Spirit is something that often happens after baptism. This is because the Spirit takes charge of our prayer; and to do such, we must be completely yielded to Him. When we pray in the Spirit, the Holy Spirit gives the utterance. Therefore, we can pray in our understanding and also in another tongue (**1 Corinthians 14:15**).

Not so long ago, I realized that there were things I received from God, which I could not recollect praying for. And in accordance with **Matthew 7:7** and **Jeremiah 33:3**, I inquired of the Lord. He answered and said, *"you prayed for those things when you were praying by the help of My Spirit,"*—praying in tongues. Clearly, I didn't know what I was praying for, but the Holy Spirit was making sure my prayer was right, to produce the right results. To be clear, there are things that God does for us out of His mercies; however, the principle is that for us to receive things from God, we must ask for it in prayer.

Contrary to many beliefs, the devil does not know everything. He only has agents in strategic places to gather crucial information. In many cases, when we pray in the Spirit, the devil and his cohort have no idea what we are asking God. We might not even understand our prayer unless the Holy Spirit interprets it. This is because *if we pray in tongues, our spirit is praying, but we don't understand what we are saying* (**1 Corinthians 14:14 NLT**); hence we *are speaking mysteries* (**1 Corinthians 14:2**). This is God's way of encrypting our conversation with Him.

You might be asking; how do I know what I am saying is good or bad? Faith, which is our way to please God, is the answer (**Hebrew 11:6**). This is an act of faith in God; we are trusting the Holy Spirit to pray the will of God on our behalf. Therefore, when we pray in the Spirit, we are pleasing God. Apart from praying the right prayers, praying in the Spirit also helps us to grow our faith. **Jude 1:20 NKJV** says, *"But you, beloved, building yourselves up on your most holy faith, praying in the Holy Spirit."* When we pray in the Spirit, we commune via yielding to the Holy Spirit. We do not necessarily understand what we are saying, but the Holy Spirit is in charge (**1 Corinthians 14:14**). This is nothing but faith in action. We simply believe that we are praying for the right things. The moment we start seeing results without praying in our understanding, our faith increases in God.

Tongues

I vaguely explained this earlier, but I feel the need to write separately about this. I had to sit down with my spiritual father, and with the help of the Holy Spirit, I got the right understanding of this. As I have earlier mentioned, tongues simply mean languages. In **1 Corinthians 13:1 NKJV**, Paul said *"though I speak with the tongues of men and of angels."* Other translations, such as the New Living Translation, rendered tongues as languages. Hence from the insight of Apostle Paul, we see that there is the language of men and angels. This means that when we are operating in the Holy Spirit, we can speak, pray or sing in the language of men or angels.

Furthermore, everything that can be done in any of our languages can be done with the tongues given by the Holy Spirit. For example, we can speak, read, write, pray and study in our language; these are also possible in the language given by the Holy Spirit. However, it is important to note that the Holy Spirit is the mastermind behind this. He is the one that will give the ability to speak, read, write, pray and read, as He pleases.

Another important thing to mention about tongue is this. As a teacher, I have noticed children of God sometimes speak the same tongue over and over. Some may even know what their tongue sounds like. Depending on the situation, it can either be good or bad. Here is why!

It can be good because, firstly, the person is a novice at speaking in tongues. Imagine when a kid begins to talk, they start with a simple word and keep on repeating it in every situation. However, as they grow, they pick up more words to express themselves. This is also applicable in tongues. Secondly, in some human languages, there are some words that have the same spelling and pronunciation but have different meanings. For example, in English "its" and "it's" had the same pronunciation, their letters are the same, but they mean different things. "Its" is a possessive determiner used to say that something belongs to something, whereas "It's" is a contraction of "it is" or "it has." The same is applicable to some words of tongues given by the Holy Spirit.

It can be bad because the person has knowingly or unknowingly memorized certain words of the Spirit. Maybe at the early days of their tongue-speaking, certain words kept coming, and now they have owned those words. The danger here is this: they've refused to grow into other words to express themselves. They are like a child stuck on the first word they spoke. To mitigate this, all that must be done is to depend on the giver of the tongues. It is not your language, so why stress your brain to speak it. In accordance with **1 Corinthians 14:14,** our mind is blind and fruitless when we are speaking in tongues. Unless the Holy Spirit gives us the interpretation, our mind is too small to comprehend it. The Holy Spirit can be trusted, let loose and let Him fill you up.

I understand that many of us like to be in charge and understand what we are saying. This just connotes a lack of faith. As a child of God in this predicament, all you have to do is ask God for forgiveness and grace—pray that God will increase your faith and help your unbelief.

6

Growth and Sustenance

In this chapter, we will discuss how to receive the Holy Spirit, commune with Him and increase our access in Him. Like my father in the Lord likes to say, the Holy Spirit is like google, He knows everything and all things. He is our internal navigator. However, just like google, it is important that we know when, how and what to ask if we want to get the right answers. Just like we carry smartphones that are connected to the internet everywhere we go, so is our spirit when we have the Holy Spirit. Nothing good comes without a guiding principle to follow; likewise, there are guiding principles to receive, sustain and grow in the Holy Spirit.

How Do We Receive the Holy Spirit?

Before we start this discussion, there is a fallacy I will like us to tackle.

Genesis 2:7 NLT — *Then the LORD God formed the man from* the dust of the ground. He breathed the breath of life into the man's nostrils, and the man became a living person.

John 20:22 NLT — Then he breathed on them and said, "Receive the Holy Spirit."

These scriptures can be misconstrued by some people as evidence that we all have the Holy Spirit. This trend of thought is not completely accurate. Yes, it is the power of the Holy Spirit that brings us life and keeps us alive (**Romans 8:11**). However, being physically alive is not indicative that we have the Holy Spirit in us. When the Holy Spirit comes, everything that is dead must come to life. When Jesus raised Lazarus from the dead, there was no indication that Lazarus received the Holy Spirit (**John 11:38-44**); even though, it was through the power of the Holy Spirit in Jesus that Lazarus was raised back to life.

Many have qualified the power of the Holy Spirit like electricity, this is because the nature of electricity is very similar to that of the Holy Spirit. To help us understand better, imagine you just purchased a new battery-powered electronic device; usually, the manufacturer will recommend that you fully charge the device before its first use. This is very similar to what happened to Adam in Genesis. When God breathed into Adam, He anticipated a full lifetime connection. Adam was charged for the first time. God's design was that we will be connected to His power source at all times. He also designed a standby mode into our being, in the event we got disconnected from His power source. However, when Adam sinned, we were disconnected from our godly charging port (**Genesis 3**). Consequently, we were all thrust into a standby mode with minimal functionality; though we were alive physically, we were dead spiritually. The fact we are still alive today is indicative of a sufficient first charge (the breath of life) and a standby charges that we receive from the Holy Spirit. This is the rudiment of the power of the Holy Spirit. His power activates our spirits and then charges us to sustain us in the standby mode—i.e. To keep us alive till we die.

Some people have either knowingly or unknowingly sort alternatives outside God to bridge the gap of disconnection. However, due to the fact that the standby charge in us is from God, the breath of God in us will always long for God. This is why there is a supernatural consciousness in every one of us, either saved or unsaved (**Ecclesiastes 3:11**). You are aware of the supernatural, whether you choose to believe it or not, it doesn't change the truth. Deep down inside, as long as you are alive, there is a longing for the supernatural. And until you fill that void with God, that longing will never go away. Unfortunately, some people have tried to suppress the longing for God within them by using diabolic powers (e.g., occult, enchantment, fraternity, new age and demonic meditation), instead of going to God. On that note, you are putting unnecessary work on our spirit to stay alive outside of God.

The Holy Spirit is God and as such we can only receive Him only through God. This simply means we do not have access to the Holy Spirit, unless through God. What we saw at creation, which is what every one of us received, is a one-time charge of the Holy Spirit. We received the Holy Spirit from God, and it is the Holy Spirit that connects us to God. However, it is the salvation work of Jesus (God the Son) that made this possible.

1 Corinthians 15:21-22 NLT, emphasis added — *So you see,* *just as death came into the world through a man, now the resurrection from the dead (from standby mode to functioning mode) has begun through another man. Just as everyone dies because we all belong to Adam, everyone who belongs to Christ will be given new life.*

We see that the first people put us on standby, but through Jesus, we are back to full functioning mode. Therefore, when Jesus breathed on His disciples in **John 20:22**, He was taking them off the standby mode into the functioning mode. Apostle Peter said in **Acts 2:38 NLT**, *"Each of us must repent of our sins and turn to God, and be baptized in the name of Jesus Christ for the forgiveness of our sins. Then we will receive the gift of the Holy Spirit."*

The Process

As explained in Chapter 2, Jesus died for our sin. In this way, He made it possible to go from standby to functioning mode. To activate the work of Jesus in our lives there are two things that must be done.

Romans 10:9-10 NKJV — *If you **confess** with your mouth the Lord Jesus and **believe** in your heart that God has raised Him from the dead, you will be saved. For with the heart one **believes** unto righteousness, and with the mouth **confession** is made unto salvation.*

As we can see, the first step to receiving the Holy Spirit is to confess with our mouth and believe in our hearts. To genuinely confess Jesus as Lord means to submit to Him. Doing this will mean acknowledging that we need Him to take charge of our life. We outrightly know that we have ruined things, we recognize the need for a change, and we want to repent of our sins. This was what Apostle Peter meant in **Acts 2:38**.

1 John 1:9 NLT — *But if we **confess** our sins to him, he is faithful and just to forgive us our sins and to cleanse us from all wickedness.*

The purpose of confessing our sin (**1 John 1:9**) is not to bring shame on ourselves, rather it is to acknowledge that we have sinned and fallen short of God's glory (**Romans 3:23**). Remember, God is omniscient and He already knows all of our sins (**Psalm 69:5**). However, confessing our sins helps us to realize we really need Jesus to help us. And in so doing we are acknowledging Jesus as the best option and allowing Him to take the reins of our life. By declaring Him as our Lord and savior, we are publicizing it so that every demon rescinds their claim over our life. Confessing our sin also helps solidify what is happening on the inside of us. On the other hand, believing is a thing of the heart. If we genuinely confess our sin and declare Jesus as Lord, chances are that we already believe in our hearts. This is because *what you say (confess) flows from what is in your heart* (**Luke 6:45b NLT, emphasis added**).

Due to these two main requirements, the children of God over the years have come up with a prayer. With the help of the Holy Spirit, this prayer envelopes these requirements. It is often called the sinner's prayer. Again, this is not to shame anybody, but to acknowledge our change. To say, yes, I was once a sinner before this prayer, but after this prayer, I am no longer a slave to sin. This prayer is therefore a turning point. I called it the new converts' prayer. If you have made the decision to let God take the wheel of your life, so that you can move from a standby mode to a functioning mode, here on earth, please say this prayer below:

Dear heavenly Father,

I thank you for sending Your son Jesus to die on the cross for my sins. I acknowledge that I am a sinner in need of forgiveness and a savior. I confess the Lord Jesus. I believe that Jesus died for my sins and God raised Him from the dead. I confess my sins and I ask You for forgiveness. I repent and turn from my sins and I invite You to come and dwell in my life. Jesus, I accept You as my personal Lord and Savior. From this day forward, I will serve, obey and trust You, my Lord. So, help me God in Jesus name. Amen!

Congratulations! You are now born again into the family of God. You now have a dose of the Holy Spirit. So, expect some subtle convictions. Please save the date for your record. It is your spiritual birthday. Please find a local church that believes in the power, the move, the baptism and the person of the Holy Spirit and join them. As a member of God's family, "we are encouraged *not to forsake the assembling of ourselves together, as is the manner of some, but exhorting one another, and so much the more as you see the Day approaching.*" (**Hebrews 10:25 NKJV**).

Once we've prayed the prayer above, this doesn't mean that everything will change overnight. It simply means that Jesus will take charge henceforth. In the words of my father in the Lord, "*don't worry, relax and continue living your life, and watch God in action.*" The most important thing is that we must be willing to yield to God at all times, for His work to come to fruition in our lives.

You may ask how do I know I am saved? *We live by believing and not by seeing* (**2 Corinthians 5:7 NLT**)*, since we know he* *hears us when we make our requests, we also know that he will give us what we ask for* (**1 John 5:15 NLT**). This is the only prayer from an unbeliever that God hears. As a matter of fact, the prayers of an unbeliever may not be answered by God, if it isn't the prayer of salvation (**Psalm 66:18**). For those who are saved, be rest assured that He hears you. I am confident because He wants all men to be saved (**1 Timothy 2:3-4**). And by doing this, there is a party in heaven (**Luke 15:7 & 10**); therefore, rejoice, today is a day of joy. You have just been translated from darkness to light (**Colossians 1:13**).

Next Step

It is important to understand what happens after we take the step to accept Jesus as our Lord and Savior. Just like every other thing, if there are no guiding principles in place, relapse is inevitable. Due to this imminent danger, I would like us to go through some things—what to expect and how to deal with it.

Many shy away from receiving Jesus because they think once they get saved there are dos and don'ts to follow. Though this is somewhat true, it is not the point. As my spiritual father described it, thinking about this in this nascent stage is like a young child thinking about bills and other adult responsibilities. Don't worry about all that, you'll eventually mature into it. These are things for adults; for now, enjoy your childhood in Christ.

In light of this, I strongly suggest that you get the book "Now that you are born again, what next? by Emmanuel

Adewusi." It will help you enjoy your childhood in Christ and debunk misconceptions.

A Dose of the Holy Spirit

As I have explained earlier, once we accept Jesus, we have the Holy Spirit in us. As such, we should expect certain things. However, these things might not be as profound as we may have heard others talk about it. This is because the level of the Holy Spirit in us at this early stage may be deemed low. In other words, we are babies in Christ (**1 Corinthians 3:1**). As babes, our level of the Holy Spirit will correspond with that. For example, we may start having non-sinful, Bible-conforming, spontaneous, and problem-solving thoughts about things. This could be the mode of communication being established by the Holy Spirit. Your conscience also comes alive; therefore, you may start to have frequent second thoughts about sinful things, this again might be the conviction of the Spirit. Dreams, visions, perceptions and many more can start manifesting at a steady minimum rate. All these are possible modes of communication from the Holy Spirit.

We must also understand that it is our spirit that is connected with the Holy Spirit (**Romans 8:16**). So, we must consciously subject our soul and body to what the Spirit is saying. We do this by obeying the instructions of the Holy Spirit. I have noticed people say, I want to obey, but I don't know if what I heard was God or not. My answer is this: what does it matter? As long as the instruction is not sinful or against the word of God in the Bible, do it. As per the scriptures, we must test all spirits (**1 John 4:1**). Once we have tested the spirit and confirmed it could be God, we are better off doing it. It is absolute obedience that allows growth in God. The more we obey, the more the manifestations of the Spirit increases. Jesus said in **John 14:15 NLT**, "*if you love me, you will obey my commandments.*" In **John 14:23 NLT**, *Jesus said, "All who love me will do what I say. My Father will love them, and we will come and make our home with each of them."* Therefore, obedience is the key to growth in God.

Read the Bible Daily

Due to the importance of obedience, there are things we can do to enhance our obedience. This includes reading, studying and meditating on the word of God. If we are to obey God, we must know His commandments. The commandments of God and everything we need to know about God is all enveloped in His word. This is why I highly recommend you read the word of God daily. Start with the gospels, preferably the gospel according to John, then go to Luke, Matthew and Mark. The reason behind this order of reading is this. These four books are the eyewitnesses' accounts of Jesus' life. The four books were written by Jesus' inner circle. Therefore, we can say these are Jesus' biography. John was known as the beloved; he had a special relationship with Jesus. So, reading the book of John first might show us some of the best sides of Jesus. Luke was very detailed and thorough, followed by Matthew, and then Mark. Once we've read all these, we can listen to the inner voice of the Holy Spirit to lead us to what book of the Bible to read next. But just as we cannot go a day without food, so we should never go a day without reading the word. What food is to the body, the word is to the Spirit.

Once we have the word of God in us, we can easily locate the voice of God and obey with certainty. Because the voice of God will naturally cling to the word of God in us (**John 14:26**). In this day of many voices, knowing the voice of God will help us navigate through many voices. One of the ways we test all spirits is by putting what was said on the scale of the written word of God—the Bible. There is something I do whenever I believe I've gotten something from God. I always ask for at least two or three scriptures to back up the revelation. This is because in the mouth of two or three witnesses the truth is confirmed (**2 Corinthians 13:1**). If it is the Spirit of God, He will always give those scriptures or the interpretation/correlation from the Bible. But if I don't get the backing from the Bible, I ignore it.

Another way we bond with God through His word is meditation. The Bible advises this in **Joshua 1:8**. What this means is to set time apart to think deeply about the word of God. Navigate the spirit realm by bringing everything in you to a standstill. Force yourself, if need be to think about the word of God. This is a very crucial part of our growth. As we do this, we will start to hear God speak back to us and expound on things. Until we are still, we cannot know our God thoroughly (**Psalm 46:10**).

There are many things that knowing the Bible will help us with. But for the sake of our study, we are only focusing on the aspect of helping us to know God.

Pray Daily

Communing with God through prayer is another key to growth. From the account of the Bible, Jesus taught His disciples one thing explicitly, and this was how to pray (**Luke 11**). It is a known fact that the one you communicate with on a regular basis, you bond with. This is the logic behind prayer. When we pray, we are communicating with God; the more we do this, the more we bond with Him. There is a myth about prayer that must be thwarted—prayer must last for several hours. This is not just wrong but actually makes no sense. There are times that several hours of prayer is needed. However, in communing with God always, here is my suggestion. Find the perfect time that you know you can consistently spend with God. This can be any time of the day and any length of time. The logic behind this is this. You will bond more with the one you speak with every day for 5 minutes than the one you speak with for 5 hours once every few weeks. The key in our communion with God is consistency.

Another point that must be made here is this. Prayer is a communion; this means it is a mode of communication. Therefore, it can be two-way. We should not always be the only one talking; we must also listen to hear back from God. This is how we communicate. In fact, spare some of your prayer time to hear back from God.

Find a Church and Be Baptized in the Holy Spirit

Due to the danger of having the wrong foundation at this early phase, finding the right church and shepherd (Pastor) is very important. Your most important criteria are a local church that believes in the Holy Spirit, His fruit, gifts and His ministry. Don't just look for a church out of convenience or to fulfill all righteousness. Ensure you find the right one for the right growth. Pray and ask God to lead you. Book an appointment if needed; explain what you have learned from this book and how you have given your life to Jesus. You are fine if they understand, and what they are saying aligns with some or all of our discussions in this book. Most importantly, whatever you are told must align with the Bible (ensure you ask for biblical references, if you do not know, and confirm it later). Like I have done in this book over and over again, there is nothing new under the sun (**Ecclesiastes 1:9**). If a revelation cannot be backed by the Bible in any way, shape or form, it is not from God. Otherwise, continue on your search. If all these criteria are met, then you have yourself a local church. All you have to do is to submit to the leadership and tell them your intention to grow in God. Let them know you will like to be baptized in the Holy Spirit with the evidence of tongue. I am sure they will help you to achieve this goal.

Sustenance

And do not bring sorrow to God's Holy Spirit by the way you live. Remember, he has identified you as his own, guaranteeing that you will be saved on the day of redemption. (**Ephesians 4:30 NLT**)

From the scripture above, we know what can bring sorrow to the Holy Spirit—the way we live. A life that pleases God is a life that is growing and thriving in God. The only way we can please God is to obey His commands. When we obey Him, we love Him (**John 14:15**); when we disobey Him, we grieve Him (**Psalm 78:40**).

So, whether you eat or drink, or whatever you do, do it all for the glory of God. (**1 Corinthians 10:31 NLT**)

Another thing we can do to ensure we are sustaining our walk and growth is to always live our lives to bring glory to God. No matter what we do, our sole goal and purpose are to bring Him glory.

Don't be impressed with your own wisdom. Instead, fear the LORD and turn away from evil. (**Proverbs 3:7 NLT**)

One of the beauties of our God is that He is love (**1 John 4:8**) and a consuming fire (**Hebrews 12:29**). Borrowing from my father in the Lord again, "the fear of God is like living life as if God does not forgive." This will not just help us grow, it will bond and preserve us in God. We will remain pure and holy until we meet Him face to face. We will be God's friends, or shall I say besties, because *the LORD is a friend to those who fear him, and He teaches them his covenant* (**Psalm 25:14 NLT**).

7

Conclusion

In **Romans 8:14,** the Bible says *for all who are led by the Spirit of God are children of God.* If I am reading this right, the Bible is saying we are not considered a child of God until we yield to the leading of the Holy Spirit. What? Yes, this is why the Holy Spirit is the most important person of our time. Here is the fact, based on this verse, it is very possible to be saved and not be considered a child of God. This is because it is the leading of the Holy Spirit that qualifies us as God's children. Remember, we cannot know His will or be convicted of sin without the Holy Spirit (**John 16:8**). What can land you in hell may not land me there. There are explicit sins highlighted in the Bible, but there are other kinds of sins that are not explicit. We must understand that to whom much is given, much is expected (**Luke 12:48**). It is only the Holy Spirit that knows our capacity. It is simply impossible to please God without the Holy Spirit. Without Him, we do not have any frame of reference with God. Therefore, if we are not God's children, are we really qualified for heaven? I don't think so.

This is because our salvation is retained and sealed by the Holy Spirit (**Ephesians 1:13**). We see that without the Holy Spirit, we can lose our salvation; and as such heaven is not attainable. So, if a person is saved but they are not being led by the Holy Spirit, I will question their salvation. You may love Jesus, but if you are not led by Him, He does not know you. In this way, being saved through Jesus is only the way in. We must advance from that entry point and grow in our intimacy with God through the Holy Spirit.

As I have earlier alluded to, though God wants every one of us to be saved and for all to have a relationship with Him (**1 Timothy 2:4**), God will never force His way on us. We must yield our desires to Him.

Our Desire

Here is another fact—in the spirit realm, there is no vacuum of power. I am sure we are conversant with the saying, "there is no vacuum of power". When two powers collide, the inferior yields to the superior. However, there are instances where the superior may yield to the inferior. Do you know that it is possible for the power of God to yield to demonic power in some cases? This is possible and it is solely dependent on the individual involved. For example, if a person is possessed by a demon, the power of God can expunge it or yield to it, depending on the person's willingness and desires. Therefore, we cannot be filled with the Holy Spirit unless we desire Him. The Bible said *"I stand at the door and knock. If you hear my voice and open the door, I will come in, and we will share a meal together as friends."* (**Revelations 3:20 NLT**). The Holy

Spirit will not force His way into us, we must yield to Him for Him to come in. The disciples in **Acts 2**, waited on God for the release of the Holy Spirit. Their waiting was an indication of their desire. We must also desire and wait on God in prayers, so He can baptize us with His Spirit.

The Holy Spirit is the promise of God (**Acts 1:4**) and yet, there are so-called Christians today without the fullness of the Holy Spirit. Why? This is not surprising because accepting the promise is a matter of our desire. Adam said, *"it was the woman you gave me who gave me the fruit, and I ate it."* (**Genesis 3:12**). In other words, what you gave me that I never asked for pushed me to sin. Therefore, the Lord said in **Matthew 7:7-8 NLT**, *"Ask, and it will be given to you; seek, and you will find; knock, and it will be opened to you. For everyone who asks receives, and he who seeks finds, and to him who knocks it will be opened."* Until we desire and ask, we are not entitled to this promise.

Furthermore, let's say a person was delivered from the devil in a setting where the presence of God was engaged. We would think that because the Holy Spirit delivered the person, He has the right to automatically enter the person. Right? Well, in the kingdom of God, things are not done this way. We must still desire God and want Him (**Matthew 12:43-45**). He gave us free will and wants us to exercise it. On the other hand, in the kingdom of darkness, a higher power only replaces the lower power. For example, a person battling with a demon may be delivered by another demon. In reality, such a person only traded a lesser demon for a more terrible one. Therefore, there is nothing free from the devil. Only God blesses and gives without adding sorrow (**Proverbs 10:22**).

The Holy Spirit will never force Himself on us. So, before or after a person is delivered, they should be encouraged to accept Jesus. This is because for such deliverance to be permanent, the person must be in Christ and be sealed by the Holy Spirit.

Take Action

"Remember, it is sin to know what you ought to do and then not do it." (**James 4:17 NLT**). I find this verse of the Bible very interesting. This is because it reminds me of the cops mirandizing a person they wanted to arrest. The Miranda warning intrigued me: "You have the right to remain silent because whatever you say or do can be used against you in the court of law." Why? Because whatever you say can implicate you in the case. You don't know the charges they have against you, and what you say might be the biggest evidence for their case.

Remember, the cops are agents of the government and in this case, they are working against you. In the same way, the devil is always working against us. Remember, the devil is our accuser (**Revelations 12:10**). So, knowing something and not doing it puts us in the category of the wicked servant (**Matthew 25:14-30**). God has entrusted us with the knowledge enveloped in this book. Not taking action as highlighted is simply hiding the treasures that He has given to us. In this way, it will not yield any return in us. This can be used against us by the devil, and it is, therefore, a sin. What we know and do not implement is very capable of killing us spiritually. Please take the right actions by inviting Jesus into your life today, obey God and be baptized in the Holy Spirit continually; this way, we are not kicking against God's way today. May God bless you.

Contact the Author

If you have been blessed by this book, it will be my joy to hear from you. You can let me know how this book impacted and influenced your life. I can be reached at info@eagboola.com. For more information about me, please visit my website at www.eagboola.com.

God Bless you.

About the Book

The intention of this book is to introduce us to the most important person today. It is a proven fact that relationships are part of life. And building the right ones gives us an even better chance of success. However, we are humans and feeble. This means today we are here and tomorrow we are gone. So, the person we know today might not be helpful tomorrow. But do you know that there is a person who lives forever, He is always there and never disappoints those in relationship with Him? This is the one we are focusing on in this book. The following, among many other mysteries, were discussed.

- The Identity: There is a proverb that says "the one who promises to make us look good, must first be examined." We explored this by looking into His nature, His acts, His ways and His track record. This was done because if we think this person is so important, these facts must prove it. What makes Him so special?
- Understanding the Person: Once we uncover the identity, it is very important to understand how we can re-

late. Is He reachable for us? What does He like and what He does dislike? What is in it for us?
- Building a Lasting Relationship: The moment we realize this person and His nature, it will be unfathomable not to want a relationship with Him. Therefore, the roadmap to building our relationship must be discussed and understood. How to build, grow and sustain this relationship becomes very important.
- A deeper dive into the most awesome relationship we can think of. Everything we think is impossible is literally possible with this relationship. His backing makes us untouchable, and drastically turns our lives around for good.
- And many more mysteries.

If such a person exists, won't you want to know? Follow me as we are introduced to the best relationship you can ever imagine. May God bless and open the eyes of your understanding as you read in Jesus' name. Amen.

Ebenezer Agboola is a teacher in the body of Christ. The core of his call is to "bring the light of understanding into the darkness of deception by teaching the word of God." He believes that ignorance is bondage and understanding is freedom. The source of all understanding is the Holy Spirit (2 Corinthians 3:17). Hence his passion to see people seek understanding and apply it properly (wisdom). This nature of his call makes him relevant not just to Christians, but to everyone.

He is the founder of a teaching ministry called *The Ministry of Light international (MOLI)*. The ministry organizes conferences and teaching events as led by the Holy Spirit; where Ebenezer serves as the host minister.

Ebenezer is happily married to Tumininu, and together they are building a family-centred on pleasing and thoroughly obeying God.